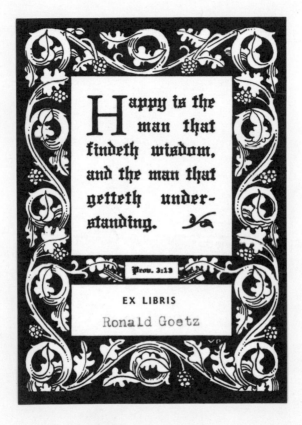

Happy is the man that findeth wisdom, and the man that getteth understanding.

Prov. 3:13

EX LIBRIS

Ronald Goetz

THE GOOD SOCIETY

The B'nai B'rith Jewish Heritage Classics

SERIES EDITORS: David Patterson · Lily Edelman

Already Published

THE MISHNAH
Oral Teachings of Judaism
Selected and Translated by Eugene J. Lipman

RASHI
Commentaries on the Pentateuch
Selected and Translated by Chaim Pearl

A PORTION IN PARADISE
AND OTHER JEWISH FOLKTALES
Compiled by H. M. Nahmad

THE HOLY CITY
Jews on Jerusalem
Compiled and Edited by Avraham Holtz

REASON AND HOPE
Selections from the Jewish Writings of Hermann Cohen
Translated, Edited, and with an Introduction by Eva Jospe

THE SEPHARDIC TRADITION
Ladino and Spanish-Jewish Literature
Selected and Edited by Moshe Lazar

JUDAISM AND HUMAN RIGHTS
Edited by Milton R. Konvitz

HUNTER AND HUNTED
Human History of the Holocaust
Selected and Edited by Gerd Korman

FLAVIUS JOSEPHUS
Selected and Edited by Abraham Wasserstein

*Published in cooperation with the Commission
on Adult Jewish Education of B'nai B'rith*

THE GOOD SOCIETY

Jewish Ethics in Action

Selected and Edited by

NORMAN LAMM

The Viking Press · New York

First published in 1974 by The Viking Press, Inc.
625 Madison Avenue, New York, N.Y. 10022
Published simultaneously in Canada by
The Macmillan Company of Canada Limited
SBN 670-34653-5
Library of Congress catalog card number: 73-12852
Printed in U.S.A.

UNESCO Collection of Representative Works, Israel Series
This book has been accepted in the Israel Series of the Translations
Collection of the United Nations Educational, Scientific and Cultural
Organization (UNESCO).

ACKNOWLEDGMENTS

Holt, Rinehart and Winston, Inc.: "The Kerchief" by S. Y. Agnon,
translated by I. M. Mask from *The Jewish Caravan,* selected and edited
by Leo W. Schwarz. Copyright 1935, © 1963, 1965 by Leo W. Schwarz. A
somewhat altered version of Lucy S. Dawidowicz's translation of "The Old
Man of Slobodka" by M. Gerz from *The Golden Tradition,* edited by
Lucy S. Dawidowicz. Copyright © 1967 by Lucy S. Dawidowicz. Reprinted
by permission of Holt, Rinehart and Winston, Inc.

KTAV Publishing House, Inc.: From *Faith and Doubt* by Rabbi Norman
Lamm.

Rabbi E. Oshry: From *Mi-Maamakim* by Rabbi E. Oshry.

The Soncino Press Ltd.: From *Horeb* by Samson Raphael Hirsch.

Vallentine, Mitchell & Co. Ltd.: *The Palm Tree of Deborah* by Moses
Cordovero.

Yale University Press: From *The Book of Acquisition,* translated by Isaac
Klein, © Copyright 1959 by Yale University Press.

Rabbi Shelomah Yosef Zevin: "Ziknah" from *Le'Or Ha-Halakah.*

Thanks to the Morris Adler Publications Fund of B'nai B'rith's Commission
on Adult Jewish Education for making the Jewish Heritage Classics Series
possible as a memorial to the late Rabbi Morris Adler, former Chairman
of that Commission.

To my children,
Chaye, Joshua, Shalom, and Sara,
who have helped their parents strive to make of
their home a good society in miniature

Do not say *yahid* [individual, solitary];
say *yahad* [together]. No one is alone.
A man is bound up with his fellows even without knowing it.
When a friend dies, a piece of our soul dies with him.

—ELIEZER STEINMAN,
Sefer Ha-aleph-beth

Preface

This volume comprises an exploration of the Jewish concept of the good society in its broadest sense. It begins with the individual and what Judaism requires of him vis-à-vis his relations with other individuals. Part II deals with the family as a microcosm of society in which specific behavioral roles are set forth for its members. The concluding section presents a cross-section of requirements for the good society, concluding with the universal yearning for peace.

No single volume could hope to do justice to so central a theme in Judaism as man's behavior in society, or the variety of forms and expressions in which that theme is expressed in the vast tradition. Yet many of the most characteristic Jewish concerns are illustrated by the specific topics chosen for presentation here. Their echo and re-echo in so many different genres of Jewish literature, created in so many different periods up to and including our own, and by so many different kinds of personalities, attest to their all-pervasive influence.

I am grateful to my daughter, Chaye Lamm, for her help with the manuscript, and to Micha F. Oppenheim for assistance in preparation of the reading lists.

N.L.

Contents

THE GOOD SOCIETY

Introduction

The Talmudic sage Rava compressed his understanding of the human condition into four Hebrew words: *O havruta o mituta,* "Either companionship or death." Without the possibility of human relatedness, man is empty. Without an outside world of human beings, there can be no inside world of meaningfulness. Personality, liberty, love, responsibility—all that makes life worth living—depend upon a community in which man can locate and realize himself.

But man is more than the sum of his connections with others. There must be a self in order for there to be communication; there must be an inner existence to relate to the outer world. If man is not an island, neither is he a switchboard, a maze of wires that transmits the messages of others but has nothing of its own to say. God created man from the dust of the earth and blew into his nostrils the breath of life, man became "a living soul" (Genesis 2:7). Onkelos, the Aramaic translator of the second century C.E., renders that phrase "a speaking soul." Speech is the vehicle of relationship. Man is a composite of soul and speech, of self and a society to whom that self relates. Without "soul" or self, he is no more than an elaborate cybernetic mechanism, lacking content or meaning. Without "speech" or social relations, he is only a species of protoplasm, so withdrawn he might as well be dead.

For man to be man he must maintain the delicate tension between self and society, between personal privacy and public relationships. Mediating between them is the family. Judaism is concerned with all three aspects of man's existence. It addresses itself to the question of his psychic and spiritual life, his dignity and destiny. But its major concern is with the quality of man's relationships to the world around him, and these are usually developed within the family.

This emphasis on family and community may best be understood in terms of the way Judaism treats the very beginnings of man. The Bible offers two accounts of creation, each giving a complementary insight. In the first, a rather general report, things are created day after day until we come to man, who is seen as part of the natural order. True, he is singled out as created in the "image" and "form" of the Creator; but he is essentially accepted in his natural settings: his lust for power, his reproductive function, his hunger and his appetites. God commands him, "be fruitful and multiply, fill the earth and master it" and rule over its creatures. Within this context, not only is man's creation good, but "God saw all that He had made, and behold it was very good" (Genesis 1:31).

The second account of creation sees man in a very special light, as a truly *human* being, separate from the rest of nature. Here the Bible no longer says what it had regularly said about the rest of creation, "Behold it was good." Instead it offers a judgment on man's condition and terms it *lo tov*, "not good." "The Lord God said, it is not good that man should be alone. I shall make him a helpmeet for him" (Genesis 2:18). What was "not good" was man's lack of human companionship. As man he could not be fully satisfied by communion with the rest of nature. Elevated and thus alienated from the other creatures, he was placed in a position of exploitation and manipulation vis-à-vis nature. With non-human nature he could not form genuine relationships. Only society can satisfy man's craving for relating to someone outside himself; thus woman was created. The bond between husband and wife thus offers a model for all human relationships.

Two things stand out in this Biblical description of the origin of man's need for society: the use of "good" in relation to man's social inclinations, and the recognition that more than a relationship with God is required to satisfy man's need for social contact (and goodness).

At first blush the verse "it is not good that man should be alone" seems only a judgment on man's welfare: it is bad for him to be lonely, it is better for him to enjoy the companionship of other humans. But the Torah intends more than this. The structure of the Hebrew verse contains a sense of the meaning of goodness which runs through all of Judaism's teaching on man's responsibilities to others—his immediate family and the larger family of man.

The Hebrew word *tov,* as well as its synonym *hesed* (one of the most difficult words to translate), implies the quality of giving. Goodness is givingness, generosity. A good person gives of himself, his goods, his talents to others. He is effluent. Goodness is functional and relational; it must therefore be seen in terms of what a person does with and to others rather than what he is inside of and by himself.

Thus, "God is good" means that He gives existence or life or happiness where there was none before. David put it succinctly: "The Lord is good to all, and His compassion is upon all His creatures" (Psalm 145:9). A modern commentator, R. Yaakov Zevi Meklenburg, reinterprets the Biblical refrain after every step of creation, *ki tov,* to mean not "that it was good" but "because He is good." It is because God is good that He creates. Jewish mysticism, the Kabbalah, is also aware of this idea. It acknowledges *hesed* as one of the ten divine *Sephirot,* or emanations, and assigns to it the function of God's effluence, His creativity, His overflowing goodness. Similarly, Plato, in *Timaeus,* teaches that God brought the world into being because He was not envious; He did not begrudge existence to those other than Himself.

Jewish law (Halakhah) incorporates this understanding of goodness into practical affairs. For example, a person is required to offer a blessing upon acquiring a new possession. If the acquisition is something that benefits only the new owner, he recites the *She-heheyanu,* thanking God "who has kept us alive and sustained us and brought us to this day." But if the item is one he can share with others, such as a house or automobile, he blesses God as *ha-tov ve-ha-metiv*, "who is good and does good." Not only is God good by giving us this or that possession, but He does good by instructing us to let others benefit from it as well. There is no goodness without generosity.

Since man was created in the divine image, that is, he resembles his Maker, he must always strive to be Godlike. Since, like God, he possesses the potentiality of goodness, he must give in order to be true to his nature. But how? And what? And to whom? Unlike God, man cannot create *ex nihilo*. To God, the Creator of all, he can give nothing; he can only return what he has received. To mute nature he cannot give out of love and compassion; he can only own and manipulate—with restraint and with wisdom perhaps, but not with the satisfaction which comes from giving personally to one like himself. So long as Adam was alone, his propensity for goodness was doomed to frustration. With no wife to love, no family to provide for, no persons in distress to whom he may show mercy, no companion whose joy and grief he can share, man cannot be good. Goodness can exist only when there are other human beings. The words of the Torah may thus be translated: "There can be no goodness as long as man is alone."

Human companionship is thus the prerequisite to goodness, the necessary condition for being human. This approach of Judaism is in marked contrast with certain widely accepted modern views. Freudian theory views man as brutish, with society censoring him and sublimating his drives. Rousseau believed that man in his primitive state is endowed with a nobility which is corrupted by a society which is inevitably evil, distorting and perverting man's essential nature. Unlike Freud, Judaism holds that man possesses an inner core of Godlike goodness. And unlike Rousseau, Judaism does not condemn society as totally evil, even while recognizing its imperfections. Rather, Judaism holds that society makes it possible for man to be good by doing good. The presence of other men elicits his goodness, sometimes discourages it, but always challenges it. Without relationships with others, man is no longer—or not yet—man.

This distinctive Jewish attitude toward family and society is so important that even God, as it were, cannot do for man what the human community can. From the very beginning of his creation, though man has a relationship with God, his reservoir of goodness is released only in a relationship with equals; only thus can he attain mutuality and reciprocity. Goodness is actualized not merely by giving but by giving out of personal relationship and acknowledgment of the other as a kindred being.

In truth, Judaism regards the "good" life primarily in social terms of ethics rather than worship. The *hasid* (the saint, the man of *hesed* or goodness) is primarily one who is generous in character and self-renouncing in his relations with others, rather than one who is only meticulous in his purely "ritual" duties. This becomes apparent in the complex interplay between the two major types of duty imposed upon the Jew: toward God and toward his fellow man. Judaism demands both without distinguishing between them, as can be seen in the constant interlacing of both types of commandments throughout the Torah. Exodus 22 and 23 are typical, and Leviticus 19 is especially noteworthy.

Yet it is no simple matter to determine how Judaism evaluates the man-man duties vis-à-vis the man-God obligations. Man's social responsibilities derive their ultimate validity from the divine law, yet there is a certain independence about them. Thus, on the one hand, the authority for man's duty toward family and society lies in the fact that God is the Lord: "And you shall love your neighbor as yourself; I am the Lord" (Leviticus 19:18). It is God who validates and commands neighborly love. On the other hand, the Talmud clearly implies that the man-man relation is in a measure independent of the man-God relation. Thus it rules that fasting and prayer on Yom Kippur absolve only the sins of man against God, not his sins against his fellow man. These latter can be forgiven by God only when the sinner has made restitution of the wrong and obtained forgiveness of the offended individual. An even more striking example of the autonomy of social ethics is to be found in the rule that applies when the person sinned against has died before the offender could apologize. Even then it is not enough to ask God's forgiveness. Rather, the Talmud requires the offender to assemble ten people at the grave of the one he wronged and declare, "I sinned against the Lord God of Israel and against So-and-so, whom I injured" (Babylonian Talmud, *Yoma*

87a). Only then will God forgive him. In Judaism assault against another human is not just a refracted sin against God: it is also an independent and autonomous transgression against a fellow mortal.

This equating of sins against man with sins against God underpins the Jewish concept of goodness. A purely "religious" sin is an act of disobedience, a failure to discharge an obligation to an infinitely higher Power. An offense in the realm of social ethics is a failure of goodness, a refusal to give in order to relate with an equal.

This is not to say, however, that Judaism conceives of man's duties to his fellow man exclusively on a one-to-one basis. Each man must relate responsibly to the collectivity as well—to family, to community, to state, to all humanity. These obligations to society, though perhaps less precisely defined, are no less significant. Admittedly, it is often difficult to distinguish between individual and social ethics because they are strongly interrelated. Unless individuals act morally in their own homes, how can there be a stable, moral society? Judaism has often been contrasted with other religions because of its intense community concern, its care for the disadvantaged, and its experience in holding together a widely scattered people.

To many observers, Western man grows progressively more individualistic. Our culture often seems to regard the single human being as the source of all truth and worth, the touchstone of all value. Nation and society appear as almost artificial conglomerations whose rules individuals may feel free to flaunt when their self-interests are threatened or curtailed. Such a radical attitude, so different from the more balanced view of previous ages, would appear to be a cultural bias without particularly compelling reasons to commend it. It is equally possible to view national or ethnic groups, for instance, as the important units and regard individuals merely as differentiated members of a collective organism. When "We the people of the United States" declared independence from England, they did so not as a collection of single Americans limited in time and space; they spoke as a corporate whole and included Americans yet unborn and states not yet admitted into the Union. Similarly, when the Torah was given to Israel at Sinai, that covenant committed all Jews in every age, for each Jew is a member of that indivisible entity called Israel. This is what Jewish tradition meant when it asserted that the soul of every Jew in every generation was present at Sinai and consented to the terms of the covenant. This does not mean that Judaism forces Jews to choose between the individual and the collective as the major source of value. Rather, it is a reminder that man is a single person and a member of a group.

The question of man's goodness, of his relationships, therefore includes other individuals and the various social forms created by the human family. Jewish tradition often considered them interchangeable. Thus, all men must feel responsible for each individual. "All Israelites are guarantors one for the other" (Babylonian Talmud, *Shevuot* 39a), and the life or death of a single human being is as important as the survival of the entire world (Babylonian Talmud, *Sanhedrin* 37a). Goodness is neither exclusively individual nor purely social, but both at once.

PART ONE

The Individual

1. What Is Required

What does Judaism have to do with man's behavior? Everything. While the Jewish sources do not tell us explicitly how to improve the world in all its various aspects, the whole of Jewish teaching is directed to guiding man's deeds and actions.

Why behave decently? Why live the moral life? Why build the good society? In Judaism these philosophical questions are formulated more practically: What does the good life consist of? What should man do or refrain from doing? What does right conduct consist of?

Both sets of questions have one basic response in Jewish tradition: God is the exemplar. Because God is ethical, man must be ethical; God sets the norms for human rectitude.

The theme of God as the model for human conduct is one of Judaism's most fundamental teachings. Usually this implies that man is called on to study the Torah in order to learn how God acted in specific situations in Scriptural history, and he then can incorporate these qualities into his own life. For example, the Rabbis bid us clothe the naked because the Lord provided clothing for Adam and Eve after they became aware of their own nudity. We must visit and nurse the sick, even as the Lord visited the patriarch Abraham when he was recuperating from his circumcision.

THE PALM TREE OF DEBORAH
Moses Cordovero

R. Moses Cordovero, a leading member of the sixteenth-century Safed brotherhood of mystics, went one step further and thus gave the theme of God as man's model its fullest and most beautiful expression. For Cordovero, man must penetrate beyond God's act which we know from the Torah to the attitude that informs it, and then make that disposition part of his own character. For instance, we must forgive one who offends us because it is in the nature of God to sustain the sinner at the very time of his transgression. We must not only forgive, therefore, but develop a personal character that will be forgiving and never vindictive.

As his surname implies, Cordovero's family came to Safed from Cordova, with other victims of the Spanish Inquisition. In the space of a short lifetime—forty-eight years, from 1522 to 1570—he became a prolific author, writing some thirty works, some of which are still in manuscript.

The slim volume from which the following selection is excerpted is Tomer Devorah (The Palm Tree of Deborah); *its origin is the verse (Judges 4:5) "and she sat under the palm tree of Deborah," but the relevance of the title to the contents is obscure. The book is a mystical-ethical treatise, a gem of Jewish moral teaching.*

It is Cordovero's thesis that knowledge of God's nature implies ethical duties for man. The deepest levels of faith lead irresistibly to the ennoblement of the most ordinary activities of man.

Since the passage is based on mystical themes, it is important to realize that the Kabbalah speaks of two aspects of God: En-Sof *(Infinite), God in His utter transcendence, above any concern or care, about which nothing can be said; and the world of the* Sephirot, *the ten spheres, or emanations, through which the* En-Sof *relates and reveals Himself to any existence outside Himself. Ultimately, the* En-Sof *and* Sephirot *are two aspects of One, Indivisible Reality.*

Indeed, this doctrine of the Sephirot, *of God as knowable, is extremely complex. It forms the major subject matter of the Kabbalah.*

The dynamic movement of the Sephirot, *of God, as it were, has the most significant consequences for man. The reverse is true as well: man's actions and conduct influence what happens within the* Sephirot. *God and man are engaged in a most profound dialogue, each deeply affecting the other. The idea of the "imitation of God" in the Kabbalah is therefore more comprehensive and intense than elsewhere in Jewish tradition. Man must not only emulate God's individual actions, but must live so as to evoke the proper harmony among the* Sephirot, *that is, in God Himself. Man mirrors God in his own life and, by proper living, he brings unity and balance to the divine life of the* Sephirot.

In this passage Cordovero seeks to explain the nature of the very first of God's Sephirot, *the holiest of all: the "Supernal Crown," containing within itself thirteen forms of mercy. From each of them he draws ethical standards for human behavior. Mercy is seen as the root quality of righteous living, intimately linked to justice and uprightness. It is a powerful force, not only enabling one to bear human infirmity but simultaneously requiring one to improve the faulty; not only making possible a society in which the righteous must live with the wicked, but at the same time requiring one to move it on to fuller righteousness.*

Cordovero states his major premise in the opening paragraph. Man is created in the image of God, which means that he can resemble the Creator. It is when man imitates God in his real life that he does resemble Him, that he fulfills the image and in effect becomes Godlike.

In order to achieve goodness, a society and its members have to be in communion with the source of goodness—with God. To put it another way, to be good, a society must strive to be more than good; it must aspire to be holy. And holiness is attained when men, individually and collectively, embody Godly qualities and virtues in their daily lives. That is why Jewish communities traditionally referred to themselves as a kehillah kedoshah—*a holy congregation.*

God's "image" and "form" refer to His deeds, not to any bodily form. In order, therefore, for man to fulfill the image of God in which he was made, he should strive to imitate his Creator in His deeds. If he does so, he enters into the mystery of God's form; otherwise he debases it. Therefore, it is proper for man to imitate the deeds of the Supernal Crown, the highest of the ten *Sephirot,* the first of the impulses or stages by which God in His infinity turns outward and becomes revealed. The deeds of the Supernal Crown are the thirteen highest attributes of mercy hinted at in the following verses by Micah (7:18–20):

> Who is a God like You, who bears iniquity
> And passes over the transgression of the
>   remnant of His heritage?
> He does not retain His anger for ever,
>   Because He delights in mercy.
> He will again have compassion upon us;
> He will subdue our iniquities:
> You will cast all their sins into the depths
>   of the sea
> You will show truth to Jacob, mercy to
>   Abraham
> As You swore unto our fathers in the days
>   of old.

Hence it is proper that these thirteen * attributes, which we shall now expound, be found in man.

I. Who is a God like You?

This refers to the Holy One as a patient King who bears insult in a manner that is above human understanding. For without doubt, there is nothing excluded from His care and concern. There is no moment when man is not nourished and does not exist by virtue of the divine power which flows down upon him. It follows that no man ever sins against God without the divine energy pouring

* Some of the thirteen are not included in the excerpt.

into him at that very moment, enabling him to exist and to move his limbs. Despite the fact that he uses it for sin, that power is not withheld from him in any way. But the Holy One bears this insult. He continues to empower this sinner to move his limbs even though he uses the power in that very moment for perversity. Though this offends the Holy One, He nonetheless tolerates it. You cannot say that He is unable to withhold that goodness from man. It lies in God's power—in the moment it takes to say the word "moment"—to wither the sinner's hand or foot, as He did to Jeroboam (I Kings 13:4). It is in His power to arrest the divine flow. Had God wished, He might have said, "If you sin against Me, do so under your own power, not with Mine." Nevertheless, He does not, on this account, withhold His goodness from man, but bears the insult, continually pouring out His power and bestowing His goodness. This is an instance of tolerance and the willingness to bear insult beyond words. This is why the ministering angels refer to the Holy One as the "patient King." And this is the meaning of the prophet's words: "Who is a God like You?" He means: "You, the good and merciful, are God, with the power to avenge and claim Your debt; yet You are patient and bear insult until man repents."

This is a virtue man should make his own, namely, to be patient and allow himself to be insulted even to this extent and yet not refuse to bestow of his goodness upon the recipients.

II. Who bears iniquity

This is greater than the preceding quality. For a destroying angel is created whenever a man sins, as we have been taught: "He who commits a sin acquires a prosecutor for himself" (Mishnah *Avot* 6:13). This angel stands before the Holy One saying: "So-and-so made me." As no creature can exist without the divine flow of power, how does the destroying angel who stands before God exist? It would only be right were the Holy One to say: "I will not nourish this destroying angel; let him go to the one who made him to be sustained by him." If He were to say this, the destroyer would at once descend to snatch the sinner's soul or to cut it off.

Or the sinner would be obliged to expiate his offense in creating the destroyer by enduring suitable punishment for his sin until the destroyer is annihilated. The Holy One does not behave in this fashion. He bears the sin and endures it. He nourishes the destroyer and sustains it as He does the whole world, until one of three things happens. Either the sinner repents and makes an end of the destroying angel by the penances he inflicts upon himself. Or God, the righteous Judge, brings the destroyer to naught by bringing suffering or death upon the sinner, which clears his record. Or the sinner descends to Hell to pay his debts.

This is the meaning of Cain's plea: "My sin is too great to bear" (Genesis 4:13). Our Rabbis of blessed memory interpreted this as: "You, God, bear [that is, You nourish and sustain] the whole world; is my sin so heavy that you cannot bear it [that is, sustain it until I repent]?" This is the greatest quality of tolerance, that God nourishes and sustains the evil creature brought into being by the sinner until the latter repents.

From this a man should learn the degree of patience in bearing his neighbor's yoke and the evils done by his neighbor even when those evils still exist. So that even when his neighbor offends him, he bears with him until the wrong is righted or until it vanishes of its own accord, and so forth.

IV. Of the remnant of His heritage

Consider how the Holy One behaves toward Israel. He says, "What can I do to Israel since they are My relatives with whom I have a relationship of the flesh?" For they, the community of Israel, are the spouse of the Holy One. He calls her "My daughter," "My sister," "My mother," as our Rabbis of blessed memory have explained. It is further written: "Israel, the people near unto Him" (Psalm 148:14)—literally: related to Him, for they are His children. This is why the verse says: "To the *she'erit,* the remnant, of His inheritance." This is like the term *she'er basar,* relationship of the flesh. For come what may, Israel is His inheritance. God says: "What shall I do if I punish them? For then the pain will be Mine!" As it is written: "In all their sorrows He was afflicted"

(Isaiah 63:9). It is further written: "And His soul was grieved for the misery of Israel" (Judges 10:16). For He cannot bear their pain and disgrace, for they are the *she'erit* of His inheritance.

So it is with regard to one's neighbors. All Israel is related one to the other, for their souls are united and each soul contains a portion of all the others. This is the reason why a few who carry out the divine commands cannot be compared with a multitude doing so, for the multitude possesses combined strength. This is the reason, too, for the Rabbis' teaching: those who are among the first ten to arrive in the synagogue receive a reward equal to all who come later, even if the latecomers are a hundred in number. The number "a hundred" is meant literally, for the souls of the first ten are united in each other so that there are ten times ten, each one of the ten including one hundred souls in his own soul. For this reason, it is said, too, "All Israel are surety one for the other." Each possesses literally a portion of all the others; and when one Israelite sins, he wrongs not only his own soul but the portion which all the others possess in him. From which it follows that his neighbor is a surety for that portion.

Since all Israelites are related to each other, it is only right that a man strive for his neighbor's well-being, that he not begrudge the good fortune of his neighbor, and that his neighbor's honor be as dear to him as his own; for he and his neighbor are one. This is why we are commanded to love our neighbor as ourself (Leviticus 19:18). It is proper that a man strive for the well-being of his neighbor and that he speak no evil of him nor desire that evil befall him. Just as the Holy One desires neither our disgrace nor our suffering because we are His relatives, so, too, should a man not desire to witness evil befalling his neighbor or to see his neighbor suffer or be disgraced. These things should cause him the same pain as if he were the victim. The same applies to his good fortune.

V. He does not retain His anger for ever

This is yet another divine quality, that even when man persists in sinning, the Holy One does not persist in retaining His anger.

Even when He does maintain His anger, it is not for ever, but He allows it to abate even though man does not repent. So we find in the days of Jeroboam, son of Joash. The Holy One restored the border of Israel; though they were unrepentant calf-worshippers, He had mercy upon them (II Kings 24:25). Why did He have mercy upon them? Because of this quality of not retaining His anger for ever. On the contrary, He allows His anger to lose its force. Though the sin still lingers He does not punish but ever longs, compassionately, for man's repentance. Hence it is written: "For I will not contend for ever, neither will I bear a grudge" (Isaiah 57:16). The Holy One shows both severity and tenderness to Israel for their benefit.

This is the quality which a man should make his own in dealing with his neighbor. Even when it is permitted to chastise his neighbor or his own children, who would suffer as a result, he should, because of this quality, not persist in his rebuke or linger in his anger but make an end and not retain his ire for ever. This applies even where such anger is permissible. For instance, in the case expounded by the Rabbis on the verse: "When you see the ass of your enemy . . ." (Exodus 23:5), they explain that this enmity refers to the man who sees his neighbor commit a sin when there is no other person present so that he cannot testify against him in a court of law. In this case it is permitted to hate the sinner for the offense he has committed. But, nonetheless, the Torah says: *"Azov taazov immo,"* "You shall surely help him." The Rabbis, noting that the word *azov* means both "help" and "leave," explained this verse to mean: "Leave aside that hatred which is in your heart." It is a religious duty to encourage him lovingly; perhaps, this way of dealing with him will succeed. This is the very quality of which we have spoken: "He does not retain His anger for ever."

VI. Because He delights in mercy

I have already explained elsewhere that there are angels in a certain celestial palace whose function it is to receive the kindness done by man. When the divine quality of justice pleads against Is-

rael these angels immediately bring that kindness to the notice of
the Holy One. He then has mercy upon Israel, for "He delights in
mercy." Even when they are guilty He has mercy upon them if
they are kind to each other. As it was in the time of the destruction of the Temple when Gabriel was told: "Go in between the
wheelwork . . ." (Ezekiel 10:2). For Gabriel is the prince of justice and power, the angel of severity as opposed to kindness. Permission was given him to receive the powers of justice "from between the wheelwork." That means, the power of judgment
became so strong that it sought utterly to destroy and exterminate
Israel, for they were deserving of annihilation. But Scripture says:
"There appeared in the cherubim the form of a man's hand under
their wings." That symbolized the hand of friendship and assistance. So the Holy One said to Gabriel: "They do kindness one to
another so that even if they are guilty they shall be spared and
have a remnant." Why? "Because He delights in mercy." That is,
He delights in the mercy which Israel does one to the other and
remembers this aspect of their deeds even when they are guilty
from another point of view.

It is fitting, therefore, that man make this quality his own. Even
when he is offended or provoked, if the offender has his good
points in that he is kind to others or he possesses some other good
quality, this should be sufficient to soothe one's anger so that his
heart is pleased with the offender and he delights in the kindness
that that man does. He should say: "It is enough for me that he
possesses this good quality." How much more so with regard to
one's wife, as the Rabbis say: "It is sufficient for us that they rear
our children and save us from sin." So should he say with regard
to all men: "It is enough for me that he has shown me or another
man kindness or that he possesses this particular good quality." So
let men delight in mercy.

XI. Mercy to Abraham

These are the people who go beyond the letter of the law as did
our father Abraham. The Holy One, too, behaves toward them beyond the letter of the law. He does not invoke the power of jus-

tice, nor does He behave toward them in strict uprightness alone, but He goes beyond the letter of the law, as they do. This is what is meant by "mercy to Abraham." The Holy One behaves with the quality of mercy toward those who behave as did Abraham.

A man should make this quality his own. Although he should conduct himself with righteousness, justice, and uprightness to all men, he should go beyond the letter of the law when dealing with the good and saintly. If he is only a little patient with ordinary men, he should be exceedingly patient with these men. He should show special compassion to them, going beyond the letter of the law he follows with other men. These men should be especially important to him and exceedingly beloved. Indeed, they should be his friends.

XII. As You swore unto our fathers

There are people who are unworthy and yet the Holy One has mercy upon them. The Talmud explains the verse: "I will be gracious to whom I will be gracious" (Exodus 23:19), as meaning that the Holy One says: "I have a special treasury for those who are unworthy." There is a treasure house of grace from which the Holy One gives them an unearned gift. For the Holy One says: "Behold they possess the merit of the fathers. I have made an oath to the Patriarchs. Therefore, even if their descendants are not worthy they shall receive a reward because they are the seed of the Patriarchs to whom I have sworn. I will lead them, therefore, and direct them until they improve."

So, too, should a man behave. Even when he meets with the wicked he should not behave cruelly toward them or insult them, but rather have mercy upon them, saying: "Even so, they are the children of Abraham, Isaac, and Jacob. If they are not worthy, their fathers were worthy and upright. He who brings disgrace upon the children brings disgrace upon the fathers. I have no wish that the fathers be despised through me." He should conceal their shame and improve them as much as is in his power.

XIII. *In the days of old*

This is a quality which the Holy One possesses with regard to Israel. When, for instance, the merit of the fathers has come to an end, and they are unworthy in themselves, what does He do? It is written: "I remember for you the affection of your youth, the love of your espousals" (Jeremiah 2:2). The Holy One actually recalls all the good deeds they have done from the day of their birth. From these and all the good qualities with which the Holy One controls the world He creates a special property with which to show mercy to them. This quality embraces all others, as the Zohar explains.

So, too, should a man behave. Even when he cannot discover any excuse for the wicked he should still say, "Behold there was a time when they had not sinned. In that time or in former days they were worthy." He should recall the good they did in their youth and remember the love of "them that are weaned from the milk, them that are drawn from the breasts" (Isaiah 28:9). In this way no man will be found an unworthy recipient of goodness or unworthy to be prayed for and to have mercy shown him.

2. Loving-Kindness

Love cannot be legislated. Even the commandment "You shall love your neighbor as yourself" was understood by most Jewish commentators as directed to action rather than feeling; that is, act lovingly to your neighbor, behave as if you love your fellow man. It is not given to everyone to love, and certainly not at all times. A society cannot be built on the basis of remote and often unattainable ideals.

Nevertheless, to love in the deepest sense remains a condition of human growth. If Jewish law cannot command it, Jewish morality can demand it—and does. In every age there were those who summoned men to aspire to nobler goals, to higher moral ambitions.

Such teachers and spokesmen of Jewish morality flourished especially in nineteenth-century Lithuania, in the *Musar* movement organized by Rabbi Israel Lipkin of Salant (hence known as Rabbi Israel Salanter). This modern sage gave the teaching of Musar (a word meaning many things: morality, inwardness, self-criticism, purity) its unique direction, its organization, its ideology. More important, he raised up a number of disciples whose saintliness became legend in their own lifetimes and whose influence is still felt in contemporary Judaism.

Musar emphasized the ethical and personal aspects of the Jewish religious life; its concern with right conduct comprehended more than the relations between man and his fellow man, the area dealt with extensively by Halakhah. Musar literature also focused on the quality of the feelings toward others, toward God, and toward oneself.

Thus Musar has come to refer to a literature, a movement, and a mood. Its literary history begins with Bahya ibn Pakuda, of the early Middle Ages. The systematic study of the ensuing Musar books was central to the movement crystallized centuries later by the Salanter. Its religious and psychological mood was not a particularly happy one. In contradistinction to Hasidism, which began somewhat earlier in Russia and Poland, Musar highlighted not joy but the tragic predicament of man. It sought to draw him into a continuing awareness of his moral shortcomings, his intellectual and spiritual limitations, his existential solitude, the inner struggle between his native inclination to goodness and his grasping self. Musar was to be studied while chanting the text aloud, characteristically in a mournful tone. Sin was to be challenged by appreciating its ever-present threat and marshaling one's inner resources against it.

During the sixteenth and seventeenth centuries Musar took an especially gloomy turn. The people were called to obedience to the Law by the promise of eternal bliss in the afterlife and the threat of damnation in the horrors of Gehinom. Much of this literature is alien to the modern Jew. Folk mysticism was real to the Jew of that period in a way we can hardly appreciate. Demons were well-known characters, and their place in the hierarchy of devils was common knowledge. Who had not heard of Lilith, queen of the demons, or Samael, captain of all the dark forces? Whether they were accepted as real beings or intended as imaginative symbols of evil is irrelevant. (Chapter 15 contains a Musar text that is somewhat typical of this genre.) The important point was that evil existed, within man and without, and it had to be met at least faithfully, if fearfully.

𝅷𝅥𝅮

MUSARITES: TYPES AND PERSONALITIES
M. Gertz

One of R. Salanter's distinguished students, R. Nata Hirsh Finkel, was known as "the Old Man" of Slobodka. A poor town across the river from Kovno, Slobodka was the site of one of the great Lithuanian yeshivot of modern times, where the teaching of Musar took hold and was developed. The "Old Man" was a charismatic figure; those who knew him (he died in 1928) are still under his spell.

In this passage, M. Gertz (the pen name of Gershon Movshovich) describes "the Old Man," based on his observations while he was himself a student at Slobodka. The author, who later became a Yiddish journalist, survived World War II in Russia. He returned to Riga in 1945, but was not heard from after 1947. This memoir is excerpted from his book, written in Yiddish, Musarites: Types and Personalities. *While it covers a number of the Old Man's teachings, the most persistent of them is that relating to love and kindness.*

He never attracted anyone's notice. A simple man, he dressed plainly in a black hat and a long topcoat, like a small-town shopkeeper. His manner too was that of a common man. His jacket was often unbuttoned; he kept his hands in his trousers pockets, like a low-class villager. Only an acute eye could tell that what looked like an ordinary beard was only the top of the long pointed beard tucked deep beneath the collar of his shirt. Three times a day he could be seen at prayers in the anteroom of the yeshiva. Having prayed, he turned about, sometimes had a brief chat with someone—and he was gone. He used to disappear, quickly, sidling furtively down the street.

He kept apart from everyone in the yeshiva. Only a few students used to visit him and presumably were close to him. He was known in the yeshiva as "the Old Man" (his real name was Nata Hirsh Finkel), though his youthful face showed no sign of age. He was hale and fresh as if he were still growing, his eyes clear and limpid. A smile usually adorned his moist lips. He was the real head of the Slobodka yeshiva and of the other yeshivot in the province. He was the father of the Musar movement.

He used to say: "Walk humbly" (one of the elements mentioned by the Prophet Micah, 6:8—"It has been told to you, O man, what is good and what the Lord requires of you, only to do justice and to love mercy and to walk humbly with the Lord your God"). This means you should carry the whole world in your heart, but not let the world know of it. Do only good, for that is why you were created. But who need know about it?

This is what he preached: Man was created in the image of God. The sages say that when man was created the angels took him to be a god and wanted to worship him. The source of man is God. God was Lord of the world before even the world was created, yet God created the world. For what purpose did God do this? He did it out of great love, to bestow upon man a wide and beautiful world. Now love is a human trait, for just as God is filled with compassion, so is man—created in His image—filled with goodness. Hence if a man performs an act of loving-kindness, he does it because he must, for that is now his nature. He cannot do otherwise. He is weighed down with goodness, even before he finds someone on whom to bestow it. Hence, he does good for his own sake because he is filled with love and wants to find an outlet for it, for his own pleasure. Then why need someone else know about it?

For half a century the Old Man directed yeshivot, yet he never signed a letter, a document, any paper connected with a yeshiva. His one book, *Etz Peri* [*A Fruit Tree*] was published anonymously in 1881. He never wrote another book, for he had discovered—he said—that instead of "making books" one ought to "make people." He used to say: "My life is my book."

He taught the majesty of man. Man is great, man is good. But man must never cease striving for the higher, the better, the more beautiful. Life is a ladder on which one ascends or descends, but one never stands in one place. If one does not ascend, one descends; better, then, to go up.

He used to preach: If man is by nature noble, then why did the Torah instruct us to do good? It would be so obvious. Doing good is itself a natural human thing. Even unbelievers do good deeds and charity. This signifies, then, that we are speaking about a love for man that we would not comprehend without the Torah. For example, a wealthy man gives generously to a poor man. The poor man is pleased, yet the donor —according to the Torah—has not fulfilled his obligation. For by the standard of the poor man, benighted and vulgar, the gift was charitable. But measured against a higher standard and more sensitive taste, it was inadequate. The poor man, however vulgar and common, is God's creature. He appears to be so ordinary that you think your contribution was more than sufficient. But you know that he was created in God's image, that he is more than he appears. Then know it!

Proof from the Gemara: Rabbi Johanan said to his children: "Hire workmen for me." The children contracted with the workmen that they would pay for their work with food. But Rabbi Johanan told them to go back and stipulate exactly what he would pay, for promising merely food, even the repasts of Solomon, would not be sufficient to discharge his obligation. To be sure, hungry and exhausted workers will be happy with a chunk of meat, too, but man must be guided by a nobler concept and a richer standard than the lowly psychology of the recipient. The Old Man used to cite Abraham, our father, who slaughtered three calves for his three guests (who appeared to be poor Arabs) that he might set before each of them a delicacy, "a tongue with mustard."

Or he would preach: A man, for instance, gives to the poor as much as he can afford. He does not stint money or time to help the poor, the sick, the unfortunate. Common sense says he is a good man; that is the world's understanding. But the Torah understands love differently. If a man supports the poor and unfortunate, that itself is not proof of love for man. It is not yet proof that he has fulfilled, "You shall love your neighbor as yourself." For were the needy whom he helps rich and enjoying abundance, our man would not grieve because they were not richer and enjoying greater abundance. His benign attitude toward the poor and unfortunate, then, did not spring from love, but rather from grief and pain for the unfortunates, and therefore he befriended them. The pity which he felt for their misfortune, and which stirred him, did not spring from love for men, but because he could not be so cruel as to witness their suffering and do nothing, because his capacity for cruelty had been exceeded. Cruelty, too, has its limits. But the Torah demands love for man because man is God's creature, made in His image, because man's origin is God. This being so, you must love not only the unfortunate and tormented, but even the well fed and the haughty. If they need help of some sort, you must be prepared to help them, too. For example: In the case of a wealthy man who becomes impoverished, it is not enough to provide him with sufficient food, but you ought to give him the kind of repasts he was accustomed to when he was rich, and even a horse and carriage, if that is what he was used to. For now that he is poor, he lacks those things just as the ordinary poor man lacks bread.

One can attain this level of doing good and loving others when one goes deeply within oneself, meditates, and tries to penetrate the real purpose of man in the world. That is man's purpose in improving himself, as when he studies Musar.

The Old Man used to say: "If I knew that I could be only what I am, I could not endure it; but if I did not strive to be like the Vilna Gaon, then I would not be even what I am."

He used to say: "The Talmud teaches that there is no reward granted in this world for performing good deeds. It is like a small village which has no facilities for changing large bills. The reward for a *mitzvah* is too great for this world. After all, what are the pleasures that man can enjoy in this world? How many earthly pleasures can man delight in? Eating well, sleeping well—how much can man savor? But if he can enjoy someone else's well-being by transferring the happiness of others to himself, then perhaps pleasure is worth thinking about."

One day people noticed that the Old Man was enjoying a special meal, a kind of a private banquet. He was happy. He was beaming. Why so? No one knew. Certainly it did no one any harm—happiness is happiness.

However, those who were close to him knew that the Old Man really had something to be happy about. He had been told that a man in a far-off land, whom he did not know, had won a great prize. So the Old Man was full of joy for him. A happy occasion, a holiday, *Mazel Tov!* And so he made himself a party. . . .

We knew that he should be told only good news. We were very careful not to tell him about anyone else's suffering, because he took it too personally. Once it happened during wartime (in 1918) that the yeshiva of Slobodka had to leave its premises and move to a different town. In that town the Bolsheviks arrested the local rich man. Just several weeks before that this same rich man had chased away the collectors who had come to raise funds for the Slobodka yeshiva. When the Old Man heard about the arrest of the rich man, he was very upset and said, "Better that they should have arrested me. I am used to sparse living, he is not. Why didn't they take me?"

This is what he would teach his students: Even when you pray, you must consider your fellow man. Maybe, in some way, you are unknowingly offending him. In the midst of your ecstasy in your prayer to God, then too you must think of your friend. The Talmud tells us that Rava, when he recited the *Shema* ("Hear O Israel, the Lord our God, the Lord is one") would place his hand over his eyes. In this most solemn moment, when man accepts upon himself the yoke of the kingdom of God, when his eyes and his heart turn to all directions and above and below, indicating the sovereignty of God over all and everywhere—this time he places his hands over his eyes. Why so? The usual explanation is: to concentrate better, to avoid distractions. But the Old Man taught: Perhaps there is someone standing nearby who will find your grimaces, your facial expressions during intense concentration offensive. That is why Rava covered his face—not to cause unpleasantness to another. . . .

From time to time the Old Man would disappear. People thought he was probably at home, for where else would he be? But those close to him knew he was not at home. They began to trail him. They caught up with him just as he was setting out with a band of gypsies. His friends appealed to him: "Teach us, Rabbi, what is the meaning of this?"

"Gypsies are the most forlorn people in the world. They do not know of rest or home. They torture themselves and their families in their wretched travels. So they ought to be heartened by a cheerful mien, a friendly smile, in their roaming and wandering."

Because he believed wanderers were the most forlorn people, he used often to steal out to nearby railroad stations. There he found much work for himself—helping travelers by carrying a bag, or giving advice or comforting them with a kind word, cheering them with a chat and sometimes with a loan. The Old Man used to say: " 'You shall love your neighbor as yourself.' Just as you do not love yourself because it is a commandment, do not love him only because it is a commandment."

In winter he would rise early, cross the bridge into town, setting out for all the prayer houses and places of study, to start and stoke the ovens. He said that if the prayer houses and study houses were warm early in the morning, a coachman, a porter, or just a poor man would come in to warm up and find himself in a sanctified place. His closest friends asked him: "Rabbi, is it your business to start the ovens and carry packages?" He answered: "Even if it were as hard as you think, your argument would be unacceptable to me. The Maskilim [the 'Enlightened Ones' who sought to open the European Jewish world to the winds of modernity] demand 'light,' enlightenment. We have to bring light to humanity. But we must not forget that a light sheds light for *all,* but itself is extinguished. Otherwise it would not be a light."

Man is an angel, indeed above the angels. For when God created the world and exhibited all its creatures before the angels, they could not think of any names for them. But Adam did. Adam understood every creature's nature. He comprehended each one's spirit and their relations to one another, and to the whole community. If even one were missing, it would mar the perfection of all creation.

The Old Man treated each yeshiva student individually and differently. He approached each in a different way in order to be able to perfect him. He saw through every student, yet he never spoke ill of anyone. A human being has free will. When he did encounter resistance, he exhausted himself trying to bring such students back on the right path. When all attempts failed, he would fast. Once he said of a rebel, "He cost me dearly." His close friends understood the meaning of his words.

On Sabbaths, at twilight, between the afternoon and evening services, the yeshiva used to seem like a sinking ship. The Holy Sabbath was ending; everyone tried to retain the Sabbath tranquillity as long as he could. But the day passed, the darkness neared. The shadows grew longer and denser. The weekdays were coming. One could not light a fire or a lamp. It was too dark to read or study. Then all turned to meditation and Musar. There were those who lamented their sins aloud in sobs. Others, in order to chase away their evil thoughts, smacked the lecterns with their bare hands so hard that sparks flew. Yet others soared silently, as if on wings, and pricked themselves as if with needles:

"Envy, lust, and the pursuit of honors put a man out of this world."

"A man is one who always goes forward, who always advances."

"A man worries about the loss of his money; but money can be replaced. He fails to worry about his days; and these never return. . . ."

A black cloud crouched overhead. Men were sinking into an abyss and wanted to save themselves. The Sabbath was departing. The weekdays were upon them. Suddenly, as after birth pangs, a rap on the table and the evening service begins: "And God, being merciful, forgives transgression."

It is bearable. God is good. He will be merciful and forgive our sins. After the evening prayers, all in unison, weeping, chant the psalm *Maskil le David* (Psalm 142). Someone sings a heartbreaking melody that could move stones to tears. All present join in the recitation sadly and tearfully. Everyone sorrows and everything mourns. Suddenly the Old Man emerges from the crowd. He chants the Havdalah * with such sweetness that the

* Prayer to mark end of Sabbath and the beginning of a new week.

tension eases and the atmosphere becomes lighter, more cheerful. He moves quickly from bench to bench greeting everyone intently: "Good week."

A group begins to form around the Old Man, spreading like ripples in the water. The students surround him and wait. The Old Man leans on a lectern and begins to talk, informally, just as one chats in company.

"We know that man's greatest obligation is to submit to the yoke of God's rule. He expresses this obligation by reciting a blessing over everything that gives him pleasure. It would seem, then, that submission to God's rule is a sort of subjugation, an enslavement. The blessings appear to be a sort of tax which man must pay for his pleasures. Yet the truth of the matter is quite different. Obedience to God's will is neither enslavement nor levy, but rather the source of all pleasure. How so?

"It is man's nature to be impressed only by something new. Things to which he is accustomed do not arouse his enthusiasm or appeal to his feelings. But things he sees for the first time awaken feelings of pleasure. Hence, man cannot really enjoy the beauties of the world because he is accustomed to his surroundings. He can appreciate their pleasures only after he has missed them.

"But, in truth, all the world is a source of pleasure and beauty. Every detail of creation, every manifestation in matter, every movement in nature, can afford us immense pleasure. Man views the radiance of nature in a mass of colors. Should this not give him endless joy? Yet it does not delight him. His ears hear; his sense of hearing unites him with his surroundings. He hears every sound and echo in the creation of the world. This should, one would think, give him boundless joy. But it doesn't. For man has gotten used to sound and sight. He finds nothing new in this to awaken joy in him.

"God bestowed upon man all the senses and perfected him from the day of his birth. Therefore, man does not appreciate God's love.

"To liberate man from the paralysis of habit, to awaken his frozen senses so that he can feel the beauty of creation and the good which fills the world, our Sages prescribed the recitation of blessings. The blessings train man to be aware always that, in the words of our prayerbook, 'with goodness the Creator renews the creation every day.' This means all creation—as if everything were now created for the first time; and man, as if he were just born. The blessings teach man to reflect: a moment ago he was not yet born into the world, or was a body without a soul, without feelings, like a blind man who does not see, a deaf man who does not hear, without understanding and intellect. Suddenly God shed light upon his eyes and brought him into a new world. He opened his arms and strengthened his bones, made his ears hear and his understanding grow. How great, then, is man's happiness!

Such insights sweeten man's life. They come from pondering the blessings: 'He opens the eyes of the blind'; 'He sets free those in bondage'; 'He raises up those who are bowed down'; 'He restores life to mortal creatures.' Through the blessings man experiences the world anew. His senses expand, as if he were just born. . . ."

Everyone listens, absorbed, open-mouthed and open-eyed. Then, all of a sudden, almost unnoticed, the Old Man has vanished. He is wandering in dark, forgotten, lonely streets.

3. Compassion

The Sages taught: it is the mark of the Israelites that they are *rahamanim benei rahamanim,* compassionate people descended from compassionate people. The tradition of compassion is deeply embedded in Judaism, and it is therefore not surprising that one of the major Jewish writers of our age, Nobel Laureate S. Y. Agnon, has dealt with it in one of his stories.

THE KERCHIEF
Samuel Yosef Agnon
(Translated by I. M. Lask)

The late Samuel Yosef Agnon is a modern Hebrew writer who deliberately cultivated a style reminiscent of rabbinical Hebrew. A man of refined esthetic sensibility, his tales deal with the experiences of previous generations, bringing the Jewish past to life and drawing their power from continuity with an ancient wisdom.

"The Kerchief" is a story that can be read for the sheer delight of its consummate artistry, despite the fact that much of the charm of Agnon's Midrashic style is inevitably lost in translation.

As with Agnon's other stories, however, this one can be read on several levels; as the Rabbis remark of certain Scriptural verses, "It says: interpret me." Clearly, it speaks of sacrifice and redemption, of compassion as a way to triumph. Is Agnon giving here a version of the Akedah story (the binding of Isaac by his father Abraham, in Genesis 22), the most fundamental theme of sacrifice in the Jewish tradition, except that the roles of parent and child are reversed? Is it, perhaps, a parable of the Messiah, a hint of how we might usher redemption into the world? Or does it speak of rebuilding the relationship between God and man? We cannot be certain.

The setting seems almost too ideal. This is a closely knit family, its members utterly devoted to each other. Husband and wife especially cherish each other, undemonstratively, and parents and children enjoy harmonious relationships. Yet there are negative elements in the story—the child has nightmares when separated from his father, and the story is filled with beggars, sickness, and outcasts.

In our context, however, the conclusion is most important; the story as a whole can be taken to symbolize the power of Rahamanut, or compassion.

1.

Every year my father, of blessed memory, used to visit the Lashkowitz fair to do business with the merchants. Lashkowitz is a small town of no more consequence than any of the other small towns in the district, except that once a year merchants gather together there from everywhere and offer their wares for sale in the town's marketplace; and whoever needs goods comes and buys them. In earlier times, two or three generations ago, more than a hundred thousand people used to gather together there; and even now, when Lashkowitz is in its decline, they come to it from all over the country. You will not find a single merchant in the whole of Galicia who does not keep a stall in Lashkowitz during the fair.

2.

For us the week in which my father went to the market was just like the week of the Ninth of Ab. During those days there was not a smile to be seen on Mother's lips, and the children also refrained from laughing. Mother, peace be with her, used to cook light meals with milk and vegetables, and all sorts of things which children do not dislike. If we caused her trouble she would quiet us, and did not rebuke us even for things which deserved a beating. I often used to find her sitting at the window with moist eyelids. And why should my mother sit at the window; did she wish to watch the passersby? Why, she, peace be with her, never concerned herself with other people's affairs, and would only half hear the stories her neighbors might tell her; but it was her custom, ever since the first year in which my father went to Lashkowitz, to stand at the window and look out.

When my father, of blessed memory, went to the fair at Lashkowitz for the first time, my mother was once standing at the window when she suddenly cried out, "Oh, they're strangling him!" Folk asked her, "What are you saying?" She answered, "I see a robber taking him by the throat"; and before she had finished her words she had fainted. They sent to the fair and found my father injured, for at the very time that my mother had fainted, somebody had attacked my father for his money and had taken him by the throat; and he had been saved by a miracle. In later years, when I found in the Book of Lamentations the words "She is become as a widow," and I read Rashi's explanation, "As a woman whose husband has gone to a distant land and who intends to return to her," it brought to mind my mother, peace be with her, as she used to sit at the window with tears upon her cheeks.

3.

All the time that Father was in Lashkowitz I used to sleep in his bed. As soon as I had said the night prayer I used to undress and stretch my limbs in his long bed, cover myself up to my ears and keep them pricked up and ready so that in case I heard the Trumpet of the Messiah I might rise at once. It was a particular pleasure for me to meditate on Messiah the King. Sometimes I used to laugh to myself when I thought of the consternation which would come about in the whole world when our just Messiah would reveal himself. Only yesterday he was binding his wounds and his bruises, and today he's a king! Yesterday he sat among the beggars and they did not recognize him, but sometimes even abused him and treated him with disrespect; and now suddenly the Holy One, blessed be He, has remembered the oath He swore to redeem Israel, and given him permission to reveal himself to the world. Another in my place might have been angered at the beggars who treated Messiah the King with disrespect; but I honored and revered them, since Messiah the King had desired to dwell in their quarters. In my place another might have treated the beggars without respect, as they eat black bread even on the Sabbaths, and wear dirty clothes. But I honored and revered them, since among them were those who had dwelt together with the Messiah.

4.

Those were fine nights in which I used to lie on my bed and think
of Messiah the King, who would reveal himself suddenly in the
world. He would lead us to the Land of Israel where we would
dwell, every man under his own vine and his own fig tree. Father
would not go to fairs, and I would not go to school but would
walk about all day long in the courts of the House of our God.
And while lying and meditating thus, my eyes would close of their
own accord; and before they closed entirely I would take my
fringed garment and count the knots I had made in the fringes, indicating the number of days my father stayed in Lashkowitz. Then
all sorts of lights, green, white, black, red, and blue, used to come
toward me, like the lights seen by wayfarers in fields and woods
and valleys and streams, and all kinds of precious things would be
gleaming and glittering in them; and my heart danced for joy at all
the good stored away for us in the days to come, when our just
Messiah would reveal himself, may it be speedily and in our days,
Amen.

While I rejoiced so, a great bird would come and peck at the
light. Once I took my fringed garment and tied myself to his wings
and said, "Bird, bird, bring me to Father." The bird spread its
wings and flew with me to a city called Rome. I looked down and
saw a group of poor men sitting at the gates of the city, and one
beggar among them binding his wounds. I turned my eyes away
from him in order not to see his sufferings. When I turned my
eyes away there grew a great mountain with all kinds of thorns
and thistles upon it and evil beasts grazing there, and impure birds
and ugly creeping things crawling about it, and a great wind blew
all of a sudden and flung me onto the mountain, and the mountain
began quaking under me and my limbs felt as though they would
fall asunder; but I feared to cry out lest the creeping things should
enter my mouth and the impure birds should peck at my tongue.
Then Father came and wrapped me in his prayer shawl and
brought me back to my bed. I opened my eyes to gaze at his face
and found that it was day. At once I knew that the Holy One,

blessed be He, had rolled away another night of the nights of the fair. I took my fringes and made a fresh knot.

5.

Whenever Father returned from the fair he brought us many gifts. He was very clever, knowing what each of us would want most and bringing it to us. Or maybe the Master of Dreams used to tell Father what he showed us in dream, and he would bring it for us.

There were not many gifts that survived long. As is the way of the valuables of this world, they were not lasting. Yesterday we were playing with them, and today they were already thrown away. Even my fine prayerbook was torn, for whatever I might have had to do, I used to open it and ask its counsel; and finally nothing was left of it but a few dogeared scraps.

But one present which Father brought Mother remained whole for many years. And even after it was lost it was not lost from my heart, and I still think of it as though it were yet there.

6.

That day, when Father returned from the fair, it was Friday, after the noon hour, when the children are freed from school. This fact should not be mentioned to children. Those Friday afternoon hours were the best time of the week, because all the week around a child is bent over his book and his eyes and heart are not his own; as soon as he raises his head he is beaten. On Friday afternoon he is freed from study, and even if he does whatever he wants to, nobody objects. Were it not for the noon meal the world would be like Paradise. But Mother had already summoned me to eat, and I had no heart to refuse.

Almost before we had begun eating my little sister put her right hand to her ear and set her ear to the table. "What are you doing?" Mother asked her. "I'm trying to listen," she answered. Mother asked, "Daughter, what are you trying to listen to?" Then she began clapping her hands with joy and crying, "Father's coming, Father's coming." And in a little while we heard the wheels of a wagon. Very faint at first, then louder and louder. At once we threw our spoons down while they were still half full, left our plates on the table, and ran out to meet Father coming back from the fair. Mother, peace be with her, also let her apron fall and stood erect, her arms folded on her bosom, until Father entered the house.

How big Father was then! I knew my father was bigger than all the other fathers. All the same I used to think there must be someone taller than he—but now even the chandelier hanging from the ceiling in our house seemed to be lower.

Suddenly Father bent down, caught me to him, kissed me, and asked me what I had learned. Is it likely that Father did not know which portion of the week was being read? But he only asked to try me out. Before I could answer he had caught my brother and sisters, raised them on high, and kissed them.

I look about me now to try and find something to which to compare my father when he stood together with his tender children on his return from afar, and I can think of many comparisons, each one finer than the next; yet I can find nothing pleasant enough. But I hope that the love haloing my father, of blessed memory, may wrap us around whenever we come to embrace our little children, and that joy which possessed us then will be possessed by our children all their lives.

7.

The wagoner entered, carrying two trunks, one large, and the other neither large nor small but medium. Father looked with one eye at us and with the other at the medium trunk; and that second trunk too seemed to have eyes and smile with them.

Father took his bunch of keys from his pocket and said, "We'll open the trunk and take out my prayer shawl and phylacteries." Father was just speaking for fun, since who needs phylacteries on Friday afternoon, and even if you think of the prayer shawl, my father had a special one for Sabbath, but he only said it in order that we should not be too expectant and not be too anxious for presents.

But we went and undid the straps of the trunk and watched his every movement while he took one of the keys and examined it, smiling affectionately. The key also smiled at us; that is, gleams of light sparkled on the key and it seemed to be smiling.

Finally he pressed the key into the lock, opened the trunk, put his hand inside, and felt among his possessions. Suddenly he looked at us and became silent. Had Father forgotten to place the presents there? Or had he been lodging at an inn where the inn people rose and took out the presents? As happened with the sage by whose hands they sent a gift to the Emperor, a chest full of jewels and pearls, and when he lodged one night at the inn, the inn folk opened the chest and took out everything that was in it and filled it with dust. Then I prayed that just as a miracle was done to that sage so that dust should be the dust of Abraham our father, which turned into swords when it was thrown into the air, so should the Holy One, blessed be He, perform a miracle with us in order that the things with which the innkeepers had filled Father's trunk should be better than all presents. Before my prayer was at an end Father brought out all kinds of fine things. There was not a single one among his gifts which we had not longed for all the year around. And that is why I said that the Master of Dreams must have revealed to Father what he had shown us in dream.

The gifts of my father deserve to be praised at length, but who is going to praise things that will vanish, and be lost? All the same, one fine gift which my father brought my mother on the day that he returned from the fair deserves to be mentioned in particular.

8.

It was a silk brocaded kerchief adorned with flowers and blossoms. On the one side it was brown and they were white, while on the other they were brown and it was white. That was the gift which Father, of blessed memory, brought to Mother, peace be with her.

Mother opened up the kerchief, stroked it with her fingers, and gazed at Father; he gazed back at her and they were silent. Finally she folded it again, rose, put it in the cupboard, and said to Father, "Wash your hands and have a meal." As soon as Father sat down to his meal I went out to my friends in the street and showed them the presents I had received, and was busy outside with them until the Sabbath began and I went to pray with Father.

How pleasant that Sabbath eve was when we returned from the House of Prayer! The skies were full of stars, the houses full of lamps and candles, people were wearing their Sabbath clothes and walking quietly beside Father in order not to disturb the Sabbath angels who accompany one home from the House of Prayer on Sabbath eves: candles were alight in the house and the table prepared and the fine smell of white bread, and a white tablecloth spread and two Sabbath loaves on it, covered by a small napkin out of respect so that they should not feel ashamed when the blessing is said first over the wine.

Father bowed and entered and said, "A peaceful and blessed Sabbath," and Mother answered, "Peaceful and blessed." Father looked at the table and began singing, "Peace be unto you, angels of peace," while Mother sat at the table, her prayerbook in hand, and the big chandelier with the ten candles—one for each of the ten commandments—hanging from the ceiling, gave light. They were answered back by the rest of the candles, one for Father, one for Mother, one for each of the little ones; and although we were smaller than Father and Mother, all the same our candles were as big as theirs.

Then I looked at Mother and saw that her face had changed and her forehead had grown smaller because of the kerchief wound around her head and covering her hair, while her eyes seemed much larger and were shining toward Father, who went on singing, "A woman of valor who shall find?"; and the ends of her kerchief which hung down below her chin were quivering very gently, because the Sabbath angels were moving their wings and making a wind. It must have been so, for the windows were closed and where could the wind have come from if not from the wings of the angels? As it says in the Psalms, "He maketh the winds His messengers." I held back my breath in order not to confuse the angels and looked at my mother, peace be with her, who stood at such a lofty rung, and wondered at the Sabbath day, which is given us for an honor and a glory. Suddenly I felt how my cheeks were being patted. I do not know whether the wings of the angels or the corners of the kerchief were caressing me. Happy is he who merits to have good angels hovering over his head, and happy is he whose mother has stroked his head on the Sabbath eve.

9.

When I awakened from sleep it was already day. The whole world was full of the Sabbath morning. Father and Mother were about to go out, he to his little prayer room and she to the House of Study of my grandfather, peace be with him. Father was wearing a black satin robe and a round shtreimel of sable on his head, and Mother wore a black dress and a hat with feathers. In the House of Study of my grandfather, where Mother used to pray, they did not spend too much time singing, and so she could return early. When I came back with Father from the small prayer room she was already seated at the table wearing her kerchief, and the table was prepared with wine and cakes, large and small, round and doubled over. Father entered, said, "A Sabbath of peace and blessing," put his prayer shawl on the bed, sat down at the head of the table, said, "The Lord is my shepherd, I shall not want," blessed the wine, tasted the cake, and began, "A Psalm of David: The earth is the Lord's and the fullness thereof." When the Ark is opened on the eve of the New Year and this psalm is said, the soul's awakening can be felt in the air. There was a similar stirring in my heart then. Had my mother not taught me that you do not stand on chairs and do not clamber onto the table and do not shout, I would have climbed onto the table and shouted out, "The earth is the Lord's and the fullness thereof"; like that child in the Talmud who used to be seated in the middle of a gold table which was a load for sixteen men, with sixteen silver chains attached, and dishes and glasses and bowls and platters fitted, and with all kinds of food and sweetmeats and spices of all that was created in the six days of creation; and he used to proclaim, "The earth is the Lord's and the fullness thereof."

Mother cut the cake, giving each his or her portion; and the ends of her kerchief accompanied her hands. While doing so a cherry fell out of the cake and stained her apron; but it did not touch her kerchief, which remained as clean as it had been when Father took it out of his trunk.

10.

A woman does not put on a silken kerchief every day or every Sabbath. When a woman stands at the oven, what room is there for ornament? Every day is not Sabbath, but on the other hand there are festivals. The Holy One, blessed be He, took pity on His creatures and gave them times of gladness, holidays and appointed seasons. On festivals Mother used to put on a feather hat and go to the House of Prayer, and at home she would don her kerchief. But on the New Year and the Day of Atonement she kept the kerchief on all day long; similarly on the morning of Hoshana Rabbah, the seventh day of Tabernacles. I used to look at Mother on the Day of Atonement, when she wore her kerchief and her eyes were bright with prayer and fasting. She seemed to me like a prayerbook bound in silk, and presented to a bride.

The rest of the time the kerchief lay folded on the cupboard, and on the eves of the Sabbaths and festivals Mother would take it out. I never saw her washing it, although she was very particular about cleanliness. When Sabbaths and festivals are properly kept, they themselves preserve the clothes. But for me she would have kept the kerchief all her life long and would have left it as an heirloom.

What happened was as follows. On the day I became thirteen years old and a member of the congregation, my mother, peace be with her, bound her kerchief around my neck. Blessed be God, who has given His world to guardians. There was not a spot of dirt to be found on the kerchief. But sentence had been passed already on the kerchief, that it was to be lost through me. This kerchief, which I had observed so much and so long, would vanish because of me.

11.

Now I shall pass from one theme to another until I return to my original theme. At that time there came a beggar to our town who was sick with running sores; his hands were swollen, his clothes were rent and tattered, his shoes were cracked, and when he showed himself in the street the children threw earth and stones at him. And not only the children but even the grownups and house-holders turned angry faces on him. Once when he went to the market to buy bread or onions the shopwomen drove him away in anger. Not that the shopwomen in our town were cruel; indeed, they were tender-hearted. Some would give the food from their mouths to orphans, others went to the forest, gathered twigs, made charcoal of them, and shared them free among the beggars and poor folk. But every beggar has his own luck. When he fled from them and entered the House of Study, the beadle shouted at him and pushed him out. And when on the Sabbath eve he crept into the House of Study, nobody invited him to come home with them and share the Sabbath meal. God forbid that the sons of our father Abraham do not perform works of charity; but the ministers of Satan used to accompany that beggar and pull a veil over Jewish eyes so that they should not perceive his dire needs. As to where he heard the blessing over wine, and where he ate his three Sabbath meals—if he was not sustained by humankind he must have been sustained by the grace of God.

Hospitality is a great thing, since buildings are erected and administrators appointed for the sake of it and to support the poor. But I say it in praise of our townsfolk, that although they did not establish any poorhouse or elect any administrators, every man who could do so used to find a place for a poor man in his own house, thus seeing the troubles of his brother and aiding him and supporting him at the hour of his need; and his sons and daughters who saw this would learn from his deeds. When trouble befell a man he would groan: the walls of his house would groan with him because of the mighty groaning of the poor; and he would know that there are blows even greater than that which had befallen him. And as he comforted the poor, so would the Holy One, blessed be He, in the future comfort him.

12.

Now I leave the beggar and shall tell only of my mother's kerchief, which she tied around my neck when I entered the age of Commandments and was to be counted a member of the congregation. On that day, when I returned from the House of Study to eat the midday meal, I was dressed like a bridegroom and was very happy and pleased with myself because I was now putting on phylacteries. On the way I found that beggar sitting on a heap of stones, changing the bandages of his sores, his clothes rent and tattered, nothing but a bundle of rags which did not even hide his sores. He looked at me as well. The sores on his face seemed like eyes of fire. My heart stopped, my knees began shaking, my eyes grew dim, and everything seemed to be in a whirl. But I took my heart in my hand, nodded to the beggar, and greeted him, and he returned the greeting.

Suddenly my heart began thumping, my ears grew hot, and a sweetness such as I had never experienced in all my days took possession of all my limbs; my lips and my tongue were sweet with it, my mouth fell agape, my two eyes were opened, and I stared before me as a man who sees in waking what has been shown him in dream. And so I stood staring in front of me. The sun stopped still in the sky, not a creature was to be seen in the street; but He in His mercy sat in Heaven and looked down upon the earth and His light shone bright on the sores of the beggar. I began loosening my kerchief to breathe more freely, for tears stood in my throat. Before I could loosen it, my heart began racing in strong emotion, and the sweetness, which I had already felt, doubled and redoubled. I took off the kerchief and gave it to the beggar. He took it and wound it around his sores. The sun came and stroked my neck.

I looked around. There was not a creature in the market, but a pile of stones lay there and reflected the sun's light. For a little while I stood there without thinking. Then I moved my feet and returned home.

13.

When I reached the house I walked around it on all four sides. Suddenly I stopped at Mother's window, the one from which she used to look out. The place was strange; the sun's light upon it did not dazzle but warmed, and there was perfect rest there. Two or three people passing slowed their paces and lowered their voices; one of them wiped his brow and sighed deeply. It seems to me that that sigh must still be hanging there.

I stood there awhile, a minute or two minutes or more. Finally I moved from thence and entered the house. When I entered I found Mother sitting in the window as was her way. I greeted her and she returned my greeting. Suddenly I felt that I had not treated her properly; she had had a fine kerchief which she used to bind around her head on Sabbaths and festivals, and I had taken it and given it to a beggar to bind up his feet with. Ere I had ended asking her to forgive me she was gazing at me with love and affection. I gazed back at her, and my heart was filled with the same gladness as I had felt on that Sabbath when my mother had set the kerchief about her head for the first time.

The end of the story of the kerchief of my mother, peace be with her.

4. Love of the Stranger

A sense of concern and responsibility for others and an identification with them as human beings: these form the cement of society. But such bonds do not always guarantee a good society. Even a band of robbers, as a great Jewish philosopher once pointed out, has its own sense of mutual responsibility and companionship.

The real test of a decent, humane community lies in its attitude toward the stranger, the outsider. A good society is one which teaches its members to overcome their natural fear and hatred of the unfamiliar and to befriend the stranger.

The Torah commands us again and again, "You shall love the *ger,*" the stranger. During most of Jewish history, Jews were a minority group, living as outsiders among others. The only foreigners who entered Jewish society were the *gerim* in the technical sense: proselytes from other peoples and religions. These converts, although committed to the Jewish religion and people, were nonetheless outsiders in habit, custom, language, life-style. Often they came alone, having severed all family connections; they were therefore the most available victims of the unscrupulous, and even of ordinary, good-natured folk.

Friendship to strangers is commanded in Jewish law. The foreigner was too unprotected and vulnerable for Judaism to leave his welfare to moral preaching. Hence, Halakhah had to legislate and enforce respect for the proselyte—his property, his person, his interest. This is the substance of the ethical-legal texts that follow.

SELECTIONS (RESPONSA AND MISHNEH TORAH)
Moses Maimonides

The selection that follows is made up of four passages from the writings of the twelfth-century Spanish-Jewish Sage Maimonides (or RaMBaM, from his name Rabbi Moses Ben Maimon). The outstanding Jewish jurist of all times, a renowned physician, and Jewry's most creative philosopher, he was also the leader of the Jewish community in Egypt, where he spent most of his mature years. So great was his fame that the generations declared that "from Moses [the Lawgiver] to Moses [Maimonides] there was none like Moses." During his lifetime many Jewish communities reverently included his name in the Kaddish prayer: "May [God's] great Name be magnified and sanctified . . . in your lifetime and in your days and in the lifetime of our Rabbi Moses ben Maimon. . . ."

Maimonides wrote the first great code of Jewish law, the Mishneh Torah, a monumental achievement. In it he showed his mastery of the entire voluminous Halakhic literature from the Talmudic period to his own times, organizing it in a systematic manner, and deciding doubtful cases authoritatively. Some of the laws concerning the attitude to strangers, included at the end of this selection, are taken from various sections of Maimonides' Code.

In addition to his codification of Jewish law, Maimonides conducted a far-ranging correspondence on all matters affecting Jews —legal questions, philosophical issues, community problems. Queries were addressed to him by rabbis and other leaders in many communities, and to these he wrote his responsa, or an-

swers, in the manner of rabbis in every generation, including our own.

This section contains excerpts from two separate responsa by Maimonides on the subject of friendship to strangers. Both were written to the same man, Obadiah, a proselyte.

I. Responsum

Your teacher sinned grievously when he called you a fool for denying that Moslems were idolators. It is fitting that he ask your pardon, even though he is your master. If he will fast and weep and pray, perhaps he will find forgiveness. Was he intoxicated that he forgot the thirty-three passages in which the Torah commands us concerning "strangers"? For even if he was right and you were wrong, it was his duty to be gentle; how much more so when you were right and he was wrong! When he was discussing the issue [whether a Moslem is an idolator], he should have been more cautious not to lose his temper with a righteous proselyte and embarrass him, for our Sages said, "He who gives way to anger is considered an idolator." How great is the duty which the Torah imposes on us with regard to proselytes!

We are commanded to honor and fear our parents. We are ordered to obey the Prophets. A man may honor, fear, and obey without loving. But in the case of "strangers," we are commanded to love with the whole of our heart. Yet he called you a "fool"! Astounding! Here you are—a man who left father and mother, abandoned his birthplace and his country and its power, and attached himself to our lowly, despised, and enslaved race; who recognizes the truth and righteousness of this people's Law, and casts the things of this world from his heart. Shall such a person be called "fool"? God forbid! Not "witless" but "wise" has God called your name: you are a disciple of our father Abraham, for he too left his father and his family and came to God. And He who blessed Abraham will bless you, and will make you worthy to behold all the consolations destined for Israel; and when God shall do good unto us, He will do good unto you, for the Lord has promised good unto Israel. . . .

II. Responsum

Thus says Moses the son of Rabbi Maimon of blessed memory, one of the exiles from Jerusalem, who lived in Spain.

I received the question of the master and rabbi, Obadiah, the wise and learned proselyte. May the Lord reward him for his work and may a perfect recompense be bestowed upon him by the Lord God of Israel, under whose wings he has sought cover.

You ask me if you too are allowed to say in the blessings and prayers you offer, whether alone or in the congregation: *"Our God"* and "God of *our* Fathers," "who has sanctified *us* through His commandments," "You have separated *us*," "You have chosen *us*," "You have inherited *us*," "You have brought *us* out of the land of Egypt," "You who worked miracles for *our* fathers," and other expressions of this kind.

Yes, you may say all this in the prescribed order, and not change it in the least. In the same way as every Jew by birth says his blessings and prayers, you too shall bless and pray, whether you are alone or pray in the congregation. The reason for this is that Father Abraham taught the people, opened their minds, and revealed to them the true faith and the unity of God; he rejected the idols and abolished their worship; he brought many people under the wings of the Divine Presence; he gave them counsel and advice, and commanded his sons and members of his household after him to keep the ways of the Lord forever, as it is written, "For I have known him that he may command his children and his household after him that they keep the way of the Lord, to do righteousness and justice." Ever since then, until the end of time, whoever adopts Judaism and believes in the unity of God, as it is prescribed in the Torah, is considered a disciple of our father Abraham and a member of his household; for it is Abraham, as it were, who converted him to righteousness. In the same way as he converted his contemporaries through his words and teaching, so he converts future generations through the testament he left to his children and household after him.

Thus, Abraham is both the father of his pious descendants who keep his ways, and the father of his disciples and of all proselytes who adopt Judaism.

Therefore you should say, "Our God" and "God of our fathers," because Abraham, peace be with him, is *your* father. And in the blessings after meals you should say, "You who have bequeathed [the Land of Israel] to our fathers," for the land was given to Abraham—as it is said, "Arise, walk through the land in the length and in the breadth of it, for I will give it to you." But as to the words, "You who brought *us* out of the land of Egypt," or "You who performed miracles for *our* fathers"—these you may change, if you wish, and you may say, "You who brought *Israel* out of the land of Egypt," and "You who performed miracles for *Israel.*" If, however, you do not change them, nothing is lost thereby, because since you have come under the wings of the Divine Presence and followed the Lord, no difference exists between you and us. All the miracles done to us have been done, as it were, both to us and to you. Thus it is said in the Book of Isaiah, "Neither let the stranger, who has joined himself to the Lord, say, 'The Lord has utterly separated me from His people.'" There is absolutely no difference between you and us. You most certainly should say the blessing, "Who has chosen us," "who has given us the Torah," "who has taken us for His own," and "who has separated us"; for the Creator, may He be extolled, has indeed chosen you and separated you from the nations and given you the Torah. For the Torah has been given to us and to the proselytes, as it is written, "One ordinance shall be both for you of the congregation, and also for the stranger that lives with you, an ordinance forever for all your generations; as you are, so shall the stranger be before the Lord." Know that our fathers, when they came out of Egypt, were mostly idolators; they had mingled with the pagans in Egypt and imitated their way of life, until the Holy One, may He be blessed, sent Moses our Teacher, the master of all prophets, who separated us from the nations and brought us under the wings of the Divine Presence, us and all proselytes, and gave one law to all of us.

Do not consider your origin as inferior. While we descend from Abraham, Isaac, and Jacob, you derive from Him through whose word the world was created. As it is said by Isaiah: "One shall say, I am the Lord's, and another shall call himself by the name of Jacob."

III. Mishneh Torah: Laws of Sales (Chapter 14)

12. Just as the law forbids wronging another man in buying and selling, so is it forbidden to wrong him verbally. So does Scripture state, "And you shall not wrong one another, and you shall fear your God, I am the Lord" (Leviticus 25:17).

13. Thus, if a man is a penitent, one must not say to him, "Remember your former deeds." If he is a son of proselytes, one must not say to him, "Remember the deeds of your fathers." If he is a proselyte and comes to study the Law, one must not say to him, "Shall the mouth that ate unclean and forbidden food come and study the Law, which was uttered by the mouth of the Lord?" If he is afflicted with sickness and suffering or if he had buried his children, one must not say to him, as his companions said to Job: "Remember: whoever perished being innocent?" (Job 4:6–7).

15. Whoever offends a proselyte, whether in matters of money or verbally, transgresses three negative injunctions, as it is said, "And you shall not wrong a stranger" (Exodus 22:20), which refers to verbal deception; "neither shall you oppress him" (ibid.), which refers to monetary overcharging. Hence we learn that he who offends against a proselyte by words transgresses three negative injunctions, to wit: "And you shall not wrong one another" (Leviticus 25:17); "you shall not wrong one another" (Leviticus 25:14); "And you shall not wrong a stranger" (Exodus 22:20). . . .

17. But why is one who deceives a proselyte financially guilty of transgressing the negative injunctions referring to oral deception, and vice versa? Because Scripture has expressed both by the same unqualified term of wrongdoing; and in the negative injunction against deceiving a proselyte there is explicit reference to the two kinds of deception, i.e., "you shall not wrong and neither shall you oppress."

IV. Mishneh Torah: Laws of Character (Chapter 6)

4. To love the proselyte who comes to take refuge beneath the wings of the Divine Presence is to fulfill two positive commandments. First, because he is included among neighbors whom we are commanded to love "and you shall love your neighbor as yourself" (Leviticus 19:18). And secondly, because he is a stranger, and the Torah said "Love, therefore, the stranger" (Deuteronomy 10:19). God commanded us concerning the love of the stranger, even as He commanded us concerning love of Himself, as it is said, "You shall love the Lord your God" (Deuteronomy 6:15). The Holy One, blessed be He, Himself loves strangers, as it is said, "And He loves the stranger" (Deuteronomy 10:18).

5. Shunning of Talebearing

The power of words is everywhere acknowledged in the Jewish tradition. God created the world by speech. When Genesis says that God breathed into man and made him a "living soul" (Genesis 2:7), the classic rabbinical translator, Onkelos, renders it as a "speaking soul." God reveals Himself to man in words, the words of the Torah, and, in response, man approaches God with words.

Words are also the major instrument of contact between man and man—in all his transactions, whether intellectual, cultural, or mercantile. For men words are the means of creation, and also of destruction. They can clarify and they can confuse; they can stimulate and they can intoxicate. They may be a blessing; but they are often a curse. The heart of Jewish worship, the *Amidah,* opens with a prayer for pure speech: "O Lord, open my lips, that my mouth may declare Your praise." And it concludes with a prayer for self-control in speech: "My God, keep my tongue from evil and my lips from speaking falsehood."

Since speech is the cement of society, loose tongues can weaken its structure subtly but critically. The dangers of gossip, slander, and talebearing have been widely discussed in Jewish ethical writings.

The evil tongue (*lashon hara*) knows no cultural boundaries. A universal ailment, it is a form of psychological aggression men use to compensate for personal deficiencies. The results are inevitable: social disharmony and conflict. A few words can destroy the most intimate personal friendships, built up over many years. A phrase spoken without thought, or words scattered casually, can break the ties of trust on which community good will depends. The very fabric of society can come apart because of verbal malice or carelessness. In our own day instantaneous intercontinental communication makes one man's innuendo every other man's news.

Modern technology has also created new problems in the ethics of communication. Industries and government require information-gathering services about individuals, particularly those in sensitive positions. The moral dilemmas created by the process of informing take many forms. But what are the limits of proper inquiry? Does industry or government have the right to ask any one of us to reveal information about our neighbors in the interests of a more efficient business community or of greater national security? We may sometimes be wrong for not volunteering important data, but surely here is a time when even to cooperate under pressure is reprehensible.

The Torah says: Do not go about among your people bearing tales. This counsel echoes throughout the Bible. "Keep your tongue from evil and your lips from speaking guile" (Psalm 34:14). Specific laws concerning the various forms of gossip and talebearing are scattered throughout the Babylonian and Jerusalem Talmuds, and similar guidance is given in many of the later ethical writings.

It remained, however, for a modern sage to collect and systematize all these teachings, and bring to bear on this common social ailment an incisive intellect and encyclopedic knowledge. R. Israel Meir ha-Kohen considered *lashon hara* ("the evil tongue") a threat and danger which must be combatted in every way. The very fact that it appears so innocent makes *lashon hara* all the deadlier an enemy. It is imperative, therefore, to know what constitutes the evil tongue, its consequences, when it is prohibited, when it might be permitted, and how to decide the many borderline cases. This R. Israel Meir ha-Kohen made clear in a work that gained such immense popularity in his lifetime that he himself came to be known by the name of his book: *Hafetz Hayyim* (literally, "he who desires life," from Psalm 34:13).

HAFETZ HAYYIM: HE WHO DESIRES LIFE
Israel Meir ha-Kohen

Born in 1839 in Lithuania, orphaned at eleven, the Hafetz Hayyim married a gentle, pious woman who supported their family by running a grocery store while he studied, wrote, and taught. The only help he gave her was to keep the books; she was illiterate. Poverty marked their lives, for the Hafetz Hayyim was extremely strict, abiding by every detail of Jewish business ethics, and preferring to forgo any gain if the least question of propriety was involved.

When he was about thirty he was catapulted to fame with the publication of his book, the Hafetz Hayyim. *The text, of which this selection forms a part, consisted of the decisions of the author on all relevant questions; the accompanying notes indicated the many and often diverging sources he utilized, and evidenced his immense learning and understanding. Although the book was published anonymously, the identity of the author soon became common knowledge; subsequent editions of the work carried his name. The author gradually assumed his place as one of the real though unofficial leaders of European Jewry, and Radin, the small Lithuanian town where he lived, became a kind of shrine of Jewish ethical aristocracy. By the time of his death in 1933, at the age of ninety-four, he had become a legend throughout the Jewish world.*

What distinguishes the Hafetz Hayyim *is its unique combination of Musar (ethics, in its largest sense) and Law. Typical, classical Halakhic methodology—the kind normally used in clarifying and codifying laws of torts, kashrut, or divorce—is applied to a typical ethical subject: gossip. Here one sees clearly the classic Jewish insistence that the Law is moral through and through, and that morality, to be meaningful and effective, must be cast in the legal mold.*

Halakhah divides the prohibition of informing on a neighbor into three categories. The first and best known is lashon hara, "gossip," including any unfavorable report by one person to another about a third, even if the report is completely true. If untrue, it is called motzi shem ra, "slander." The third is rekhilut, talebearing or repeating lashon hara to its victim, thus defaming the culprit. (A tells B what C said about B.)

The second category is more or less clear. One may not slander another in any circumstances. The other two require less malice for their performance and, because the reports are not false, include a number of gray areas and borderline cases requiring clarification. The Hafetz Hayyim is thus divided into two parts: the first concerns lashon hara, and the second, from which this selection is taken, deals with rekhilut, or talebearing.

In his introduction the author comments that whereas he is analyzing the particular issue of lashon hara or rekhilut, as the case may be, technically involving only one Biblical prohibition, in actual fact gossip involves other transgressions as well. For example, if I listen to gossip, not only do I (as well as the gossiper) violate the specific commandment against gossiping, but each of us also violates the commandment "You shall place no stumbling block before a blind man" (Leviticus 19:14)—that is, by providing an audience for the gossiper, I make it possible for him to indulge in the sinful act and stumble morally. Furthermore, if I gossip about another behind his back, but in his presence pretend to be his loyal friend, I violate the commandment, "You shall not hate your brother in your heart." This is not a matter of piling up violations in order to show the author's legal virtuosity or to impress the pious reader. It is a bold act of stripping an accepted social convention in order to reveal the enormity of the evil it begets and its dreadful consequences.

Because talebearing always involves at least three people, proper names are here provided wherever the author uses only the third person singular pronoun. In keeping with traditional usage, the names of the sons of Jacob, viz., Reuben, Simeon, Levi, Judah are used. In most cases it is Reuben who is the transgressor, the talebearer. He tells Levi a tale of what Simeon did to or said about Levi, thereby antagonizing Levi toward Simeon.

Section I

1. One who informs on a friend, that is, reveals what he said to another in confidence, violates a negative commandment, as it is written, "Do not go about among your people bearing tales" (Leviticus 19:16). This is a grave sin, and can cause the death of many souls in Israel; thus the end of this verse is, "do not stand idly by the blood of your neighbor." The murder of everyone in the city of Nob illustrates this. All its inhabitants were priests but they were killed as a result of the talebearing of Doeg the Edomite (I Samuel 22). The negative commandment we have mentioned is explicit in Scripture, but talebearing also involves, indirectly, many other transgressions of positive and negative commandments.

2. Who is a talebearer? Reuben, who carries reports from Simeon to Levi, saying: "Such did Simeon say about you; such did Simeon do to you; such did I hear that Simeon did or wanted to do to you." Even though Reuben's report does not imply malice on the part of Simeon, and even though Reuben does not interpret Simeon's words or acts as malice, Reuben's act is still considered talebearing. Similarly, such informing is considered talebearing even if Simeon would not deny it if asked, either because the report is true or because Simeon feels justified in doing or saying what he did.

3. The prohibition of talebearing applies even if the talebearer, Reuben, had no malicious intention of inspiring hatred in the heart of Levi against Simeon, and even if Reuben believes that Simeon was fully justified in what he did or said. For instance: Reuben spoke or acted in a certain manner against Levi. Levi then upbraids Reuben for this, and Reuben attempts to justify himself by saying that Simeon too had said the same thing about Levi. If Reuben foresees that by saying this he unwittingly instigates Levi to resentment against Simeon, even if this is not his primary intention or desire, then this too is regarded as talebearing by Reuben against Simeon.

4. All that we have described is prohibited even if the report was absolutely true, without the least admixture of falsehood. This

is certainly so in the case where the two, viz. Simeon and Levi, were originally friendly toward each other, and Reuben disrupts their relationship by his talebearing. In this instance, Reuben is considered *rasha* [wicked], and because of this act he is regarded as most abominable in the eyes of God. So Scripture says, "There are six things the Lord hates, yea, seven which are an abomination to Him," and the last of them is "he that sows discord among others" (Proverbs 6:16–19). The Sages declared that this seventh category is the worst of all. However, even if Simeon and Levi were enemies to begin with, Reuben is guilty of the sin of talebearing if he carried a report from one to the other.

5. The prohibition of talebearing applies regardless of whether Reuben voluntarily offered the information to Levi, or whether Reuben only hinted darkly at Simeon's activity and Levi begged Reuben to tell him the whole story of what Simeon said about him. Even if this Levi is the father or teacher of Reuben, and the former pleads with the latter to repeat what Simeon said, and even if this report is to be considered only a secondary level of talebearing [see later, *Section II:2*], nevertheless it is forbidden to repeat it in any circumstances.

6. Even if one knows that by refraining from imparting the information he will suffer great economic damage, he must nevertheless refuse to engage in talebearing. Take the case where Reuben is employed by Levi. The latter insists that Reuben report Simeon's activities to him. If Reuben does not do so, he may be suspected by Levi of conspiring with Simeon and he may therefore lose his job and be unable thereafter to provide for his family. In such a case, despite this threatened loss, the talebearing is forbidden. This is the general principle concerning all negative commandments: one is required to risk losing his entire fortune in order to avoid transgressing them. This we find stated in the *Shulhan Arukh*. It is true that we are also told there that revealing information is permitted if such reporting will avoid unnecessary damage and still a conflict. Nevertheless, one should not be hasty in utilizing this dispensation for it involves a number of complicated details.

7. Certainly, if by abstaining from talebearing a man will suffer no financial loss but merely be subject to vilification and vitupera-

tion, he must not engage in it. If one finds himself in such a situation, let him pay no heed to the abuse he will experience. Let him know in his heart that because of this he will, in the hereafter, be considered as one of the lovers of God and there his radiance will be as great as the sun. For the Sages taught that those who are insulted but do not insult in return, those who hear themselves vilified but do not respond in kind, of them Scripture says, "and those who love Him shall be as the sun when it goes forth in its might" (Judges 5:31). This is certainly true of one who, as in our case, is scorned for being faithful to the commandment of the Lord.

8. How shall Reuben respond if asked by Levi, "What did Simeon say about me?" This depends upon whether Reuben can devise an answer which will not be completely untrue, and yet not fall into the category of talebearing. If he can, then he should respond in this manner, and thus avoid uttering a falsehood. If, however, he estimates that such a response will prove unacceptable, he is permitted to tell a complete lie for the sake of peace. However he may not, Heaven forbid, go so far as to swear falsely.

9. In general, Reuben may not tell Levi a story from which it will become clear to Levi that Simeon was the one involved, even if Reuben does not say explicitly that it is Simeon of whom he is speaking. The same is true if Levi knew the facts of what was said about or done to him, but did not know who said or did them. If Reuben hinted to him the identity of this person, he has violated the law against talebearing.

10. It is also forbidden to inform through a stratagem. For instance: Reuben knows that Simeon had caused Levi some harm or dishonor, and so they had quarreled with each other. Now Reuben wants to revive the old conflict in a manner that will not appear obvious to Simeon and Levi. So Reuben speaks smoothly, evasively, casually mentioning the harm or dishonor that was perpetrated long before, as if he did not even know who was guilty of doing it. He thereby causes Levi to recall what Simeon had done to him. This, and anything like it, is absolutely prohibited.

11. Know that it makes no difference whether one informs by speech or by writing. In either case, the prohibition against talebearing is violated. Similarly, the prohibition applies with equal force to bringing a report to Levi that Simeon deprecated Levi's

merchandise as to speaking ill of Levi himself. The principle in both cases is the same: Reuben, in saying what he does, causes Levi to bear enmity against Simeon.

Section II

1. It is forbidden to bear a tale to a single individual; it is certainly forbidden to relate it to many people.

2. Even the secondary level of talebearing is forbidden in all circumstances. By this is meant all such reporting as is not directly a case of talebearing but comes close to it. For instance, praising a man for charitableness in front of his partner, or the generosity of a wife before her husband. That is surely not talebearing. Yet it may lead the latter to suspect the former of taking too many liberties with the latter's money. Or take the more subtle case where Reuben tells Levi, "I asked Simeon for an opinion about you and he refused to answer me." Such an act is prohibited as secondary talebearing. That is true even when Reuben's report to Levi about Simeon lends itself to two kinds of interpretation, one favorable and the other unfavorable, and Reuben, in the way he says it, seems to incline to the unfavorable interpretation. Not only that, but even if it appears that Reuben inclines to the favorable interpretation, Reuben is forbidden to say this sort of thing if he knows Levi to be suspicious and quarrelsome, judging others adversely and tending to misconstrue what they say about him. The same prohibition is in force if Reuben knows that there is a degree of enmity between Simeon and Levi, and that Levi is looking for an excuse to quarrel.

3. Some authorities maintain that if Simeon spoke ill of Levi in the presence of three or more people, and one of them reported to Levi what Simeon had said, that this does not constitute talebearing. Their reason is that eventually the incident will become known anyway. After all, a number of people heard the original statement; one friend has another, and one reveals these things to the other. They believe the Torah forbade only the kind of talebearing wherein one reveals what otherwise would probably remain unknown. However, this interpretation involves many com-

plex details, which we have discussed above in The Laws Concerning Gossip. In effect, one ought not to rely upon this opinion. R. Solomon Luria [1510–1573], in one of his commentaries, states that many authorities, including Maimonides and the Tosafot, disagree with this opinion and forbid such reporting in all circumstances. They forbid it even if Reuben wishes to report Simeon's words about Levi to Judah; so it is certainly forbidden if Reuben wishes to report them to Levi himself.

4. Let us take a somewhat similar case. Suppose Simeon wishes to dissolve his partnership with Levi because he believes he has prospects of entering into a better partnership with others. Then, as happens, these prospects do not materialize. Reuben is forbidden to talk about this to Levi even if three or more people had heard about it, because Levi will no doubt bear a grudge against Simeon for wanting to leave him. He would feel like Jepththah who said to the elders of Gilead when they implored him to lead them in battle against the Ammonites: "Did you not hate me and drive me out of my father's house? So why have you come to me now that you are in distress?" (Judges 11:7). So too the feeling of rejection by one of the partners may cause the partnership to be dissolved, or, at the very least, he will feel distressed about it. Thus Maimonides writes that if one reports about another in a manner which will result in causing the other bodily or financial injury, or even distress or fright, such report is considered gossip [i.e., talebearing, for Maimonides often uses the two terms interchangeably]. What we have said concerning partners applies equally to all such cases, for example, a marriage match. It is forbidden to tell the prospective groom that his intended bride had wanted to marry someone else but had been unsuccessful, or vice versa.

Section III

1. It is forbidden to bear a tale even if it is the complete truth without the least admixture of falsehood, even when Simeon is not present while Reuben reports his words to Levi. It makes no difference if Reuben would say the very same thing were Simeon

present. And it is certainly forbidden if Reuben has the effrontery to tell the story in the presence of Simeon and say to his face: you said thus-and-thus about or did such-and-such to Levi. Here the sin committed is far greater than in the previous case [talebearing in the absence of Simeon], for here he implants even stronger hatred in the heart of Levi against Simeon. Now Levi will accept the report as complete truth, for he thinks that Reuben would not dare repeat it in the very presence of Simeon if it were not the complete truth. In addition to the prohibition of talebearing, this involves all three principles in a number of other serious transgressions.

2. If, in Reuben's presence, Simeon speaks ill of Levi and Reuben then repeats the story to Levi, it is then forbidden for Levi to come to Simeon and complain, "Why did you say such-and-such about me to Reuben?" The reason is that this act constitutes a new case of talebearing by Levi against Reuben. This holds true even if Levi does not explicitly mention Reuben's name but says simply, "I heard you said such-and-such about me," if it will become obvious to Simeon that Reuben is the culprit. Unfortunately many people affected by talebearing fall into the trap of carrying tales themselves.

3. Furthermore, talebearing includes more than the case in which the report is given to the victim of the story, i.e., in which Reuben tells Levi what Simeon said about Levi. Talebearing is involved even when the report is given to a fourth party, i.e., Reuben informs Judah what Simeon said about Levi. Such reports tend to circulate widely, from one man to another, and eventually cause quarrels to break out between Simeon and Levi.

[*Author's Note:* One should refrain from telling such tales even in confidence and when there is certainty that the confidence will be respected. Generally, the report concerning Simeon and Levi involves something unfavorable about one or the other of them. Thus a confidential report itself must be considered in the category of gossip. So, though it is not talebearing, it is prohibited because it is gossip.]

Certainly, Reuben may not tell Judah even in confidence what Simeon said concerning Levi, if Levi is the son or another relative of Judah. It is human nature to feel distressed about such reports about close relatives. Thus a report to a close relative, even in confidence, is considered talebearing.

4. Reuben is permitted to tell the story to a fourth party, Judah, if it is his intention that Judah reproach Simeon for speaking ill of Levi. However, he must fulfill all of the following seven conditions before proceeding:

a. Reuben must have personal knowledge of Simeon's wrongdoing, and not learn of it merely by hearsay.

b. He must not be impulsive in judging Simeon wrong, but reflect carefully on the matter before he considers Simeon guilty.

c. He must first himself reproach Simeon gently in an effort to have him improve his ways.

d. He must not exaggerate Simeon's guilt.

e. He must intend, as well, the welfare of Simeon—to keep him from further wrongdoing—and not derive any pleasure from speaking about Simeon.

f. There must be no other way of attaining this goal.

g. He must thereby cause no damage to Simeon greater than would have been caused against him had his report been accepted as valid evidence in a court of law.

Section IV

1. The prohibition of talebearing applies even when the tale contains no new information previously unknown to Levi, i.e., when Levi knows what Simeon did to or spoke about him but has never paid full attention or given serious consideration to this grievance. Now, however, Reuben provokes him to enmity by repeating the information. For instance: Levi was involved in litigation and found guilty. Reuben meets him and inquires as to the outcome of the case. Levi replies: "I lost so much and so much." Whereupon Reuben says: "The verdict was unjust." Here Levi already knows the facts, but Reuben agitates him and incites him

to new enmity toward the judge or his adversary.

2. If Simeon disparaged Levi in the presence of two people, and one of them violated the prohibition against talebearing by repeating the story to Levi, the second of the two is nevertheless forbidden to relate the same story to Levi, especially if he embellishes the tale. It is a clear violation, and the perpetrator is considered a talebearer. Certainly, if he infers from Levi that he is still undecided as to whether to accept the report of Simeon's defamation—for instance, if Levi asks him if he is sure that Simeon defamed him before the two of them—then it is obviously forbidden for him to confirm the tale. But even if he can draw no such inference, nevertheless he must refrain from revealing the incident to Levi, lest he thereby deepen the resentment of Levi toward Simeon, for Levi will give the story greater credibility when he hears it from two people than when he heard it only from one. Furthermore, this second report may lead to a quarrel by reviving the enmity caused by the first.

3. If one has transgressed this commandment and informed on a friend and now wishes to repent his sin, he has no way of making amends save by asking his pardon and pacifying him. He must also repent before God for having transgressed the negative commandment concerning talebearing.

6. Moderation

"**E**ven as men's faces differ," the Talmudic Sages used to say, "so do their opinions." It is human to be individual. It is also human to cooperate and to compromise. To incline too much to any one extreme makes us either a cause of discord or a partner in evil. Wisdom lies in moderation.

The Jewish people, like all peoples, has had great experience with this problem. Its Sages have worried about human strife, analyzed its sources, and sought to limit and moderate it. To illustrate this concern with moderation, we have chosen a collection of aphorisms, parables, and comments from Hasidism, one of the most argumentative periods in Jewish history and also one of the most religiously productive.

Hasidic leadership had a special interest in the problem of conflict. While the movement proclaimed that it had come to heal the wounded spirit of Israel, to bring joy where there had previously been dejection, and to teach the love of all Israel, its very existence created fierce strife, splitting the House of Israel into two hostile camps: the *Hasidim* (literally: pietists) and the *Mitnagdim* (literally: opponents). The latter, concentrated mostly in Lithuania, were implacable enemies of Hasidism, of its founder, R. Israel Baal Shem Tov (the Besht), and of the various *Zaddikim* who succeeded him in its leadership.

Furthermore, as the Hasidic movement itself grew, interpretations of its message began to diverge. There were many genuine differences of opinion among succeeding Hasidic masters, and these sometimes were turned into pretexts for community conflict. As a result, Hasidism was torn apart by a number of controversies. The insights of the Hasidic masters can therefore be read in the context of their own involvements in strife, and their vexation and pain because of their dilemma: a movement which preached peace and love had paradoxically aroused disharmony and enmity. Understandably, its teachers were concerned with how to live amid contention and how to overcome it.

SAYINGS OF THE HASIDIC REBBES

The sayings presented here come from the Hasidic rabbis, most of them late-eighteenth- or nineteenth-century figures. The Zaddikim, or Rebbes, are most frequently referred to not by their names but by those of the communities in which they lived or served; thus, "the Ropshitzer" is R. Naftali of the town of Ropshitz, "the Lubavitcher" the successor of the Rebbe who once lived in Lubavitch.

Only a few of the Hasidic teachers set down their teachings in writing. Most of the sayings that follow are brief insights of one or another of the Rebbes, recalled and recorded by a disciple. Since the Rebbes sought to teach the people in terms they could understand, their tales are rich in folk wisdom and yet practical; they are charming and yet realistic. They pretend to no complete answers; their insights and partial truths were mainly oral in form: short but incisive interpretations of a verse, a folksy story, an aphorism, a parable.

The opening tale of the Ropshitzer ("The Two Tablets") is typical. It sheds a good deal of light on the human situation, on the kind of dilemmas which are not open to simple, direct resolution. The way the Ropshitzer puts it evokes a deep response. He is right in what he says; but what does he mean to teach by giving problems with no solutions? Does knowing we must live in a paradox, a conflicted situation, help make it bearable and open the way for coping? The two contradictory but equally valid options open to him before birth remain counterpoised in theory only. But then, at the Mazel Tov of his birth, symbol of the entrance into the real, hard, practical world, he is faced with the cruel need for a clear choice. When man emerges from theory into practice, he must begin to live and act, and not only think, in accordance with the right way. An existential choice must be made between the two ways—but without permanently rejecting the excluded option.

The Two Tablets

The Ropshitzer declared that before his birth an angel showed him a tablet divided into two columns.

On the right he read: "In order to know the Torah, a man must have no compassion for his wife and children. If he works to satisfy their needs, he will have no time to study the Torah" (Talmud, *Eruvin* 22). On the left, opposite it, he read: "He who pities people is pitied in Heaven. A man must care for his family even beyond his strength, for their lives are dependent upon his" (Talmud, *Hullin* 84).

On the right: "The learned man should be like unto a fiery flame" (Talmud, *Taanit* 4). On the left: "Who will inherit the world-to-come? The meek and lowly one, who bows when entering and leaving" (Talmud, *Sanhedrin* 88).

On the right: "A man should be wise in his fear of the Lord" (Talmud, *Berakhot* 17). On the left: "You shall be simple-hearted before your God [a paraphrase of Deuteronomy 18:13]. If you are simple-hearted, your lot is with your God" (Midrash, *Yalkut, Shofetim*).

On the right: "Be satisfied with a minimum, like Rabbi Hanina ben Dosa" (Talmud, *Taanit* 24). On the left: "He who pledges himself not to drink wine, and thus afflicts his body, is called a sinner" (Talmud, *Taanit* 11).

The Ropshitzer gave other such examples for a while, and then said: "I was deep in thought on how difficult it is to find a way of behavior which will reconcile these contradictions when suddenly I heard a voice say: '*Mazel Tov*, a male child is born.' I remained wondering, and since then I still labor to find the way to follow both rules, however contradictory."

Unreasoning Hostility

The Ropshitzer said: "Moses led the life of a hermit and pitched his tent outside the camp. That is why his critics condemned him for exclusiveness and aloofness. Aaron, however, took pains to pacify all who quarreled and went freely among the people. He was, in his turn, condemned for being too democratic and unmindful of his high position. The opponents of a good man will blame him, no matter what his behavior."

Angels and Mortals

The Gerer Rebbe commented on the story in the Talmud (*Sanhedrin* 38) that when the Creator desired to create man, He asked the advice of the angels; some favored the plan, others opposed it. "Then," added the Rebbe, "the Lord exclaimed: 'Since even angels have differences, why not create man?'"

Opposition to the Great

The Mezeritzer said: "Let no one be discouraged by violent opposition. Robbers attack the one who carries jewels on his person, not the one who drives a wagonload of fertilizer. Like the carrier of gems, we must be prepared to repel our assailants."

Only Experts Decide

Rabbi Nachman Kossover was once an adversary of the Besht. One day he overheard several quite ordinary people talking against the Besht, and he related the following story to them:

"Two famous jewelers were working on a royal crown. A dispute arose between them regarding the proper place for a certain gem. A passerby agreed with one of the artists. Both rebuked him, saying: 'If we have an argument, it is because we are experts in the art of fashioning crowns. But you know nothing of this art, how dare you express an opinion?' "

The Lion's Trap

The Tzanzer and the Sadigurer Rebbes were involved in a long-standing quarrel. Many of the Dzikover Hasidim began to take sides. Their Rebbe, Rebbe Meier, read them the following fable from the *Yalkut:*

"A lion had to go without food so long that the breath of his mouth was no longer sweet. He met an ass, and said to him: 'Place your head near my mouth and tell me if my breath is sweet.' The ass did so and reported unfavorably.

" 'How dare you insult me?' exclaimed the King of Beasts, and promptly ate him up.

"A few days later he met a wolf, and put the same question to him. The wolf replied favorably. 'How dare you lie to me?' roared the lion, and devoured him too.

"Later he questioned a fox, but the shrewd animal was not to be caught in the trap. 'I am sorry,' said the fox to the lion, 'I have a cold and cannot smell.'

"Get yourself a convenient cold," said Rebbe Meier to the Hasidim, "and you will be saved from the lion."

The Jealous Adversary

When Rabbi Moses Teitelbaum, the Oheler, was a young man, he was a bitter enemy of Hasidism, which he considered the worst of heresies. One day he stopped at the house of his friend Rabbi Joseph Asher, who, like himself, was an opponent of the Hasidic innovations. In those days the prayerbook, according to the Sage, Rabbi Isaac Luria, whose word had been a precursor of Hasidic doctrine, first appeared in print. When the book was handed to the two teachers, Rabbi Moses tore the bulky volume out of the messenger's hands and hurled it onto the floor. But Rabbi Asher lifted it up, saying: "After all, it is a prayerbook, and should not be handled disrespectfully."

When the Lubliner heard of this, he prophesied: "Rabbi Moses will become a Hasid, but Rabbi Asher never. For he who today burns with enmity, will burn tomorrow with love of God, but the road is closed to him whose hatred is cold."

And it came to pass in truth as the Lubliner had foretold.

Insincere Peace

Said the Lubliner: "Better an insincere peace than a sincere quarrel."

Every War a Holy War?

The author of *Kol Omer Kera* said: "We read in a Midrash that Cain and Abel quarreled for the reason that each wished to establish the Holy Temple on his land. This excuse has been used ever since for every shedding of blood and for every war. People always say that they fight on behalf of a holy purpose."

Prepared for More

The Vorker and a friend were traveling on a stagecoach when they were young. His friend complained that the driver hurried and insulted them when they wished to pray with devotion. "How can you bear this so calmly?" asked the Vorker's friend.

"The reason is that I was prepared for even more insolence and abuse than we are receiving!"

Words of Kindness

The "Yud's" wife was mean-tempered and often quarreled with him. But the "Yud" never answered back with a single word. Once, however, when his wife harassed him more than usual, he replied with a few words. Rebbe Bunam asked him: "Why did you answer her today when normally you do not?"

"Because I saw that she was upset that I didn't care about her nagging," replied the "Yud." "The few words I said to her were truly a kind deed."

Accusations to Fit the Person

Rabbi Bunam learned that he had been accused of a misdeed. He turned to his Hasidim and said: "Usually accusations fit the person accused. A lowly person is accused of a low crime, a distinguished man of a higher offense. When Joseph's brothers were accused of stealing the goblet, Judah exclaimed: 'A person like me you accuse of stealing?' [Genesis 44:18 begins Judah's speech in Hebrew with the words *bi,* "me."] I may say the same: of all possible accusations, they accuse me of a crime entirely unsuited to my character!"

Leaves of the Trees

Rabbi Simon Deutsch was a conservative Hasid and greatly opposed any new system. He was responsible for the disagreement between the "Seer" and the "Yud" and later sought to break up the friendship of the Apter and Rebbe Bunam. The Apter refused to listen to him, and said: "I believe that if you were alone in a forest with no man to argue with, you would quarrel with the leaves on the trees."

The Defamation of Enemies

The Kotzker's last twenty years were passed in solitude. He hardly ever left his home, and only on rare occasions did he see his Hasidim and speak a few words to them. The enemies of the Kotzker spread false rumors about him, casting doubt upon his sanity. The Gerer Rebbe comforted the troubled disciples of the Kotzker, saying: "From the defamations by our enemies we may truly learn our Rebbe's greatness and influence. Were his interpretation of Hasidism just ordinary, it would not provoke such strong opposition. Let us follow his teachings loyally."

More Particular Than God?

The Sassover once gave his last coin to a man of evil reputation. His students reproached him for it. He replied: "Shall I be more particular than God, who gave the coin to me?"

Without Protest

Once Rebbe Shneour Zalman of Ladi, the Rav, visited a rabbi who was a *mitnaged,* an opponent of Hasidism. The rabbi told his Hasidic visitor that he had placed under the chair on which he sat the volume *Noam Elimelech,* written by the Hasidic teacher, Rebbe Elimelech.

"What sort of a man is he?" asked the *mitnaged.*

"He is the following sort of a man: even if you would place him under the chair on which you are sitting," said the Rav, "he would keep silent and not say a word in protest."

The Soft-Spoken Enemy

The Kobriner commented upon Psalm 10:10, "He crouches, he bows down, and the helpless fall into his mighty claws." In explanation he told the following fable:

"An old mouse sent her son out to search for food, but warned him to be careful of the enemy. The young mouse met a rooster and hastened back to his mother in great terror. He described the enemy as a haughty being with an upstanding red comb. 'He is no enemy of ours,' said the old mouse and sent her son out again.

"This time he met a turkey, and was still more frightened. 'O Mother,' he said, panting. 'I saw a great puffed-up being with a deadly look, ready to kill.'

"'Neither is he our enemy,' replied the mother. 'Our enemy keeps his head down like an exceedingly humble person; he is smooth and soft-spoken, friendly in appearance, and acts as if he were a very kind creature. If you meet him, beware!'"

A Loyal Wife

The wife of one of the Berditchever's enemies met the Berditchever Rebbe on the street one day and poured a pail of water over his head. The Rebbe ran to the synagogue and prayed: "O Lord, do not punish the good woman; she must have done this at the insistence of her husband, and she is therefore to be praised as an obedient wife."

The Tears

Rebbe Sussya's wife was a quarrelsome woman, and constantly urged him to separate from her.

One night he called to her and said: "Hendel, look here!" He showed her that his pillow was quite damp. Then he said: "Our Sages declared: 'If a man puts away his first wife, the very altar sheds tears over him' (*Sanhedrin* 22). Do you still want a divorce?"

From that moment on, Rebbe Sussya's wife was quiet, peaceful, and friendly.

Delay Your Wrath

The Gastininer Rebbe made it a rule never to express his displeasure with anyone on the same day he was offended by that person. The next day he would say to the man: "I was displeased with you yesterday."

Doubling a Loss

The Lubliner asked his wife to prepare his evening meal earlier than usual because he wished to have more time to do a certain good deed. It happened that supper was served later instead of earlier than usual. The Lubliner said: "I would normally scold the people of my household for disobeying me. But I wished to gain time to please the Lord. Shall I displease Him by becoming angry, thereby doubling my loss?"

The Example of Self-Restraint

Rebbe Leib Saras said: "Of what use is mere study of Torah when he who learns is proud and ill-tempered? The good man should himself be the Torah, and people should be able to learn good conduct simply by observing him."

Silence Under Provocation

Said the Kotzker: "The verse in Psalm 81:8, 'I answered you in the secret place of thunder; I proved you at the waters of Merivah' [*Merivah* means quarrelsomeness], teaches us that the Lord will answer the prayer of the man who keeps his anger secret, though provoked by the other man's quarrelsomeness."

Atonement for Anger

The Stanislaver Rebbe used to be awakened every morning by the sexton, in order to pray on time. One morning the sexton failed to call the Rebbe and he came late to synagogue. The Rebbe, who was quick-tempered, struck the sexton twice on the cheek. He immediately regretted his hasty act, and decided to atone for it by leaving the town and wandering about as a beggar for a year. When the year had ended, he returned to Stanislav, but because of his ragged garments and overgrown hair and beard, no one recognized him. He came to the synagogue and stood near the door among other poor tramps. At the end of the services he was invited to the president's home for the Sabbath meal. His behavior pleased the host, and he was invited to remain for the night. The disguised beggar awoke early and began quietly to recite Psalms.

Soon after, the sexton came to awaken the president and finding him still asleep stole the silver candlesticks from the dining-room table. Hiding them beneath his cloak, the sexton knocked at the president's bedroom door. When the latter came out, he noted at once that the candlesticks were missing and asked the sexton if he had seen any stranger about. The sexton hinted that the tramp had stolen the candlesticks. The Rebbe then asked the sexton: "Will you swear that I stole them?" This question so angered the sexton that he slapped the Rebbe's face twice. When he was about to do so a third time, the Rebbe cried out: "You owe me only two blows, and I want no interest. Return the candlesticks to their place, and tell the congregation that their Rebbe has returned."

The Control of Wrath

The Koretzer said: "Long ago I conquered my anger and placed it in my pocket. When I have need of it, I take it out."

Is Anger Permissible?

Rabbi Menachem Mendel of Lubavitch used to restrain an angry outburst until he had looked into the codes to learn whether anger is permissible in the particular instance. But how much genuine anger could he feel after searching for the authority in the *Shulhan Arukh?*

Boaz and Ruth

Said the Ropshitzer: "Anger is to be avoided in all circumstances. Had Boaz become angry at Ruth when she sought him out, he would never have married her, and King David would not have been born."

Sayings of the Bratzlaver

He who is as yet unclean and has not purified himself of inclination toward evil must not interfere with the wicked or enter into quarrel with them.

The greater a man's understanding, the further does he remove himself from quarrels.

When a man quarrels with you, do not imitate him, for then your opponent will discover that he spoke the truth about you. Revenge yourself through kind deeds toward him, and it will be proved that he lied.

Bear in mind that life is short, and that with every passing day you are nearer to the end of our life. Hence how can you waste your time on petty quarrels and family discords? Restrain your anger; hold your temper in check, and enjoy peace with everyone.

7. Courage

In order to fulfill its purposes, society sometimes demands more than material support or moral assent. It calls upon men to lay down their lives on behalf of some great principle or for the sake of their fellow men or for society itself. At such times both man and society are being tested. Are the causes for which we are summoned worthy or trivial? Is the martyrdom demanded sacred or cynical?

Equally important are questions which probe the depth of one's personal courage and his vision of himself and of life. Are we but small self-contained nomads bent solely on self-preservation, valuing only our own survival and pleasure? Or is there something beyond ourselves, some transcendent cause, some value larger than life itself, that evokes a courage whose existence we barely suspected? Indeed, does anything or anyone have the right to demand that we surrender our lives? Or are the only things worth living for those which we are prepared to die for?

Such questions are not new. Men have always faced alternatives in which personal existence had to be weighed against cherished ideals, life itself against that which makes life worthwhile. Violence, especially war, has raised the problem time and again. Self-preservation is not only an instrument but also a sacred principle;

but so too is concern for the life and well-being of one's fellow men. In every generation men have pondered how to choose between them, where to draw the line between courage and self-contempt, between cowardice and legitimate self-interest, between martyrdom and masochism.

Jewish history has had more than its share of such painful dilemmas in its thirty-five-hundred-year span. The Talmud discusses such problems in detail, and while it could not foresee every new situation in all its complexity, its interpretations offer insights and guidance for changing conditions. Because of the nature of the problems, the law sometimes offered a two-level answer: what *must* be done and what *ought* be done; a minimal Halakhic requirement, and a suggestion for greater courage and self-renunciation beyond the letter of the law, as an act of *hasidut,* or heroic piety.

QUESTIONS AND ANSWERS OUT OF THE DEPTHS
Ephraim Oshry

This selection reflects one such painful decision, focusing the Halakhic discussion on an agonizing dilemma that must have recurred hundreds of times during the Holocaust. It treats a problem involved in the victimization inflicted by sophisticated beasts, by demons in human form. When the author was asked for a Halakhic decision, he formulated a logical reasoned responsum derived from the sources with technical competence. But like other responsa in the work from which it is drawn, it is a document which simultaneously reveals the courage and the faith of certain Jews under intense duress.

The author, Rabbi Ephraim Oshry, now living in New York City, titled his collection of Halakhic case histories Sheelot U-Teshuvot Mimaamakim (Questions and Answers out of the Depths, *or* Responsa de Profundis), *referring to the verse in Psalms (130:1), "From the depths I called to You, O Lord." The author survived the "depths," where he ministered as a guide to Jews who courageously refused to yield the dignity of their faith and their high resolve to live by its precepts.*

The first excerpt, from the author's Introduction, sets the background for the question-and-answer exchange. The second is the responsum itself, presenting the decision-making process on matters of life and death.

Introduction

"My soul weeps in secret" [a reference to Jeremiah 13:17] for the Jewish people who fell by the sword of persecution and annihilation when they were delivered into the hands of the enemy who wreaked havoc with the beloved ones of Israel, mercilessly killing young and old, babies together with their mothers. A third of our nation perished before their time had come, and their spiritual strongholds were desecrated by the enemy who exterminated and murdered in the most unnatural and cruel ways, in crematoria and gas chambers. It seemed as if, God forbid, our perpetuity and hope were cut off by God.

At that time, when I was in the valley of carnage in the Ghetto of Kovno, I was privileged to serve the community, in addition to physically participating as a fellow sufferer in my brothers' forced labor. In the midst of thickening darkness and anguish, I continued to disseminate Torah in my *Bet Hamidrash* [synagogue study hall], which was widely known as "Father Ezekiel's Chapel."

After the accursed villains sealed the doom of this *Bet Hamidrash,* and wrecked it and converted it into a prison, I continued to "bless the Lord in the congregations" [a reference to Psalm 26:12] and teach Torah publicly in the "Funeral-Prayer Room." . . . In particular, I devoted myself to daily study together with the group known as *Tiferet Bahurim.* I endeavored to provide moral support for depressed Jewish young people, and tried to impart to the masses the insight that just as we thank God for the good, so too must we bless Him when we experience evil, because God is good to those who wait upon Him and hope for His loving-kindness. Therefore, we must wait silently for deliverance by

God, and fortify ourselves with faith and trust as we bear the yoke with joy; for there *is* hope. . . .

The candle of the Lord still flickered at that time. The great Sage, Rabbi Abraham Kahana Shapiro, the Rabbi of Kovno, was still alive. Although he was critically ill and lay prostrate on his sickbed, there were many who came to him seeking his Torah guidance. For this awful era gave rise to peculiar questions that were unimaginable in normal times. All these acute problems, most of them involving matters of life and death, demanded immediate solutions. Since I had been a steady visitor in his home, and a very close friend, the rabbi would ask me to study these questions and express my opinion on them.

In this manner, I collected many answers to various types of questions characteristic of this extraordinary period. I recorded them for the future, as a memorial to the suffering and agony and poverty and anguish, as a sign and symbol of the deadly sword that was drawn across the throat of the Eternal People—which, despite all this, managed to live in holiness and purity, observing the Torah. For they practiced what the Sages taught: " 'You shall love the Lord your God with all your heart and all your soul'—even if it means giving up your soul [life]."

Now, fifteen years since I recorded these responsa, I collected and collated the bits and scraps of paper which were beginning to yellow and crumble. I realized that they contained a great deal of valuable, irreplaceable historical material which presents an over-all picture of the spiritual life of the ghetto residents involved in their daily struggle for existence. I considered that "it was from God" that I had recorded these responsa, making it possible to erect thereby a memorial to the righteous and innocent Jews who sanctified the Holy Name in their lives and in their deaths.

Let this memorial serve as a remembrance and a surviving remnant of Lithuanian Jewry, a Jewish community that was rooted in its magnificent yeshivahs, its rabbis, and its distinguished scholars.

Responsum
(Volume II, No. 1)

THE QUESTION

At the very beginning of the German occupation of Lithuania, as soon as they put their bestial feet upon its soil on the 28th of Sivan, 5701 [1941], they began to manifest their great cruelty toward Jews in every malicious and barbaric way. Every day they organized manhunts in the streets of Kovno, seizing and abducting Jews, men and women, and sending them to the fearsome Seventh Fort, where their doom was sealed. In this action against the Jews, the accursed Nazis were helped by their Lithuanian underlings, who were overjoyed at this opportunity to hound the Jews whom they had always hated, to harass them and kill them and destroy them, as they had so long dreamed of doing.

Whoever troubles Israel, as the Sages taught, eventually rises to leadership. Amongst the Lithuanians were those who so excelled in brutality and savagery against the Jews, especially when they wanted to curry favor with their German overlords, that the Germans appointed them the leaders and administrators of the roundup of the Jews. The Germans were confident that they would perform their tasks loyally because of their venomous anti-Semitism, pent up within them for generations and now bursting forth like some poisonous pus. Indeed, the Lithuanians distinguished themselves in violence against and murder of their Jewish victims no less than the Germans themselves. They rounded up hundreds of Jews on the streets, dragged them out of their homes, and sent them on to their dreaded destinations. In this group of victims was included a large number of scholars of the yeshiva.

During those maddening days I was asked by our teacher, the saint and Sage Rabbi Abraham Grodzinski (may the Lord avenge his blood!), principal of the yeshiva of Slobodka, to go to Rabbi David Itzkowitz (may the Lord avenge his blood!), who was then secretary of the Rabbinical Association, and request of him to go to the Lithuanians who were in charge of this roundup of the Jews, and whom he had known from before the war, and to implore them to release the yeshiva scholars whom they had captured.

The question then arose whether, according to the Law, it was permitted for him to approach the Lithuanians on behalf of the yeshiva students. Such a mission might clearly endanger his life too, for they would abduct him, along with other unfortunates. Must he, then, endanger his own life in order to save the lives of other Jews?

THE ANSWER

There are two relevant passages in the Talmud, *Sanhedrin*. In the first (73a) we read: Whence do we know that if one sees his neighbor drowning or being attacked by a wild beast or assaulted by robbers that he is required to come to his aid? From Scripture, which teaches, "You shall not stand idly by the blood of your neighbor" (Leviticus 19:16).

The second passage (74a) tells us that the Sages decided in a famous meeting in Lydda that with regard to most of the commandments of the Torah, if one is told, "either violate them or be killed," he must violate the commandments and not submit to martyrdom. However, with regard to three commandments, one must be killed rather than violate them. These three are: idolatry, unchastity, and murder. The Talmud continues and tells us that we derive the requirement of martyrdom in the case of unchastity from the case of murder: just as I must be killed rather than kill another, so must a married woman submit to martyrdom rather than commit adultery. Then the Talmud asks: But how do we know that one must choose martyrdom in the case of murder? The answer is that it is a rational principle, which is illustrated by the story of a man who came before Raba and said: "Mari Dorai—a gentile baron of the area—said to me, kill so-and-so, else I will kill you. What shall I do?" Raba's decision was: "Let him kill you, but you must not kill. For who says that your blood is any redder than his [the intended victim's]? Maybe his blood is redder than yours." [This means: Who is to measure the relative value of two human beings? Since you cannot prove your greater value, we must assume that all human beings are equal and therefore you may not murder him to save yourself.]

Now, apparently, these two passages contradict each other. The first passage teaches us that we must endanger our lives in order to save a neighbor from drowning, a wild beast, or murderer. Yet according to the logic of Raba in the second passage, we should ask: Why so? Who says that his, the victim's, blood is any redder than mine so that I must jeopardize my life for his sake? Thus, the first passage seemingly demands that one risk his own life for the sake of his fellow man, while the second does not, on the grounds that no positive action should be taken to sacrifice one life for another.

The only way to reconcile these two passages is to say that the first one, which mandates help to a fellow man in mortal distress, speaks only of a situation in which I can save my neighbor without thereby endangering my own life. At such time I may not "stand idly by the blood" of my neighbor. However, if such assistance to a neighbor does entail danger to my life, I am not required to offer my life for him; this is the principle taught in the second passage, that there is no way of determining whose blood is redder.

Support for this interpretation may be found in the words of the *Tosafot* (*Yevamot* 53a) where the problem is raised: granted that one who is faced with the alternative "kill or be killed" must choose to be killed, because "who says that your blood is any redder than his?" However, what if one is told that he will be thrown against an infant and thus kill it, but should he resist he will himself be killed? Here he is taking no positive action in committing murder; must he resist and risk being killed instead? *Tosafot* decides that he ought not resist, for there is a difference between the case where he is called upon actively to kill another human being, and one where he is totally passive, for his body is being used as a weapon by the murderer. In this latter case, where he is not at all an active participant in the act of murder, the law cannot demand of him that he submit to death, because we reverse the question and ask: "Who is to say that his blood [the infant's or any intended victim] is redder than yours?" We must conclude that the principle of human equality [one's blood is no redder than another's] leads us to eschew any overt act of taking a life—whether killing my neighbor in order to protect myself, or suffering martyrdom by active resistance in order to save him.

Hence, *Tosafot* holds that while I may not actively take a life to save my own, I need not offer my own life in order to spare another one where I will be a passive instrument of his death. Certainly, therefore, I cannot be called upon to endanger my own life in order to save my neighbor from drowning or attack by beast or man.

In our present case, therefore, it would seem clear that we must forbid the envoy from approaching the Lithuanians, for he would thereby endanger his life for the sake of others, and this he may not do because "who says their blood is any redder than his?"

However, it may not be legitimate to compare the case of the Talmud and that of *Tosafot* to our present problem. For in their case, the question is one of entering into a situation of *clear* danger to life; and the decision was to prohibit such jeopardy in order to save another who was in equally clear danger to his life. Here, however, the problem is one of entering into a situation not of clear and definite danger, but of *possible* or *doubtful* danger. And where another person is in *definite* danger, perhaps indeed we are obliged to enter into *possible* danger to save him, on the grounds of "you shall not stand idly by the blood of your neighbor." If this distinction is valid, then in our present case we would require of Rabbi David to undertake the mission to the Lithuanians, because his situation is only one of doubtful danger to his life, whereas the yeshiva scholars are most certainly going to be killed by the wicked ones, may their name be blotted out.

However, this distinction does not seem to be valid. The commentators apparently interpret our Talmudic passages differently, and conclude that our Talmud, i.e., the Babylonian Talmud, does not require accepting possible danger to save one in definite danger. They assume that the Jerusalem Talmud does hold that one must embrace possible danger to save another from definite danger. But the leading decisors [such as Alfasi, Maimonides, R. Asher, the Turim, and *Shulhan Arukh*] do not cite this opinion of the Jerusalem Talmud, but instead insist that on the basis of our Babylonian Talmud one should not enter even into possible danger in order to save another from clear and present danger. Since these major decisors [who codified the Halakhah and decided in case of doubt or controversy], who are our most important sources of Halakhic decision, favor the Babylonian over the Jerusalem Talmud, we must conclude in our case that the above-mentioned Rabbi David ought not undertake this mission, possibly risking his life, in order to try to help the yeshiva scholars, whose lives are in definite jeopardy.

But see *Arukh Hashulhan* (*H.M.* 626:4), who cites the controversy between the Babylonian and Jerusalem Talmuds and the inclination of the Halakhic authorities to favor the Babylonian Talmud. The author then adds: "Nevertheless, each situation should be judged by itself, according to its context. One should weigh the matter very carefully and—although the Halakhah does not require risking one's life even in a state of possible danger to save others in definite danger—one should not be overconcerned with his own safety."

Similarly, we learn from the words of the Netziv (R. Naftali Zvi Yehudah Berlin), that whereas one is not *commanded* to expose himself to possible danger to save another who is in definite danger, yet it is an act of piety (*Hasidut*) to do all one can, including risking one's life, in order to save a friend who is in imminent danger of death.

From all the above we must conclude that legally the abovementioned Rabbi David need not endanger himself in order to save the yeshiva scholars captured by the enemy. However, if this Rabbi David is a man of courageous spirit, and his generosity is such that he is willing to take his chances in an effort to save the scholars, certainly we ought not restrain him. The Netziv is sufficient authority for us to rely upon in this case, especially in the light of the decision by the *Arukh Hashulhan* that one ought not be overconcerned with his own safety where he has the opportunity to save another life, for the Mishnah compares the saving of one life to saving the entire world. This is especially true in our present case of scholars of Torah, for the fate of the Torah itself is intertwined with that of the yeshiva scholars who study Torah and devote their lives to it, and particularly at a time of this sort when the intention of the enemy is to destroy not only the Jewish body but also the Jewish soul. It is for this reason that they directed such special anger and brutality toward the great Torah scholars, blaspheming the Name of the Holy One of Israel; for as is well known, they revile and curse the God of Jacob when they torture the martyred saints of our people and lead them to their extermination.

In keeping, then, with the decisions of the Netziv and *Arukh Hashulhan,* anyone with spirit and courage ought to feel obligated to do whatever he can to save the scholars so that the Lamp of the Lord, which is the light of Torah, will not be extinguished; and thereby he will also thwart the evil plans of the enemy to lay their hands upon the delight of Israel, the treasure of Torah, and to obliterate its memory from the world.

Indeed, that is what happened: the above-mentioned Rabbi David listened to my plea, girded his loins with courage, and went to the Lithuanians to plead for the lives of the yeshiva scholars. He succeeded in his efforts to release them from their imprisonment.

Remember unto him his goodness, O God, and avenge his pure and innocent blood which was spilled some time later in the death camps.

PART TWO

The Family

8. Marriage

Since society is, to a large extent, the family writ large, the quality of family life often reflects the state of society's health. The relations of husband and wife, from courtship through death or divorce, are therefore of primary concern to Judaism. The first commandment to man recorded in the Torah is "be fruitful and multiply," i.e., perpetuate the species. And the legal, moral, and psychological dimensions of marriage form a major part of the entire Talmud and its subsequent literature, from commentaries through codes.

Jewish law acknowledged the tremendous social implications of marriage by requiring that a *minyan,* a quorum of ten adult males who constitute the minimum of an *edah* (community), be present as groom marries bride before two qualified witnesses. Marriage is too important to allow it to be kept private; it is always more than a personal contractual relation. Its significance for the individuals involved, as well as its consequences for both private and public morality, also prompted the Rabbis to formulate the laws of divorce with the utmost scrupulousness.

꜀꜂꜀꜂

MARRIAGE LAWS
FROM: HOREB
Samson Raphael Hirsch

Rabbi Samson Raphael Hirsch was one of the greatest of all the expositors of traditional Judaism in nineteenth-century Western Europe. A distinguished thinker, educator, and community leader, this father of German Orthodoxy fearlessly advocated the wholeness of Jewish life and law. He taught that one could and should be totally and uncompromisingly committed to the Torah even while fully participating in Western culture, a doctrine which went by the name of Torah im Derekh Eretz. *The goal of this form of education was the development of the* Yisroel-mensch, *the "Jewhuman," one who fully realizes his Jewish obligations and his human talents. He was a separatist in community matters, and led his* Kehillah *out of the general Jewish community organization of Frankfort; remarkably, his separatist community survives to this day in many of the corners of the world to which his followers fled after the Holocaust. In recent years there has been a growing appreciation of Hirsch's thought and teachings as more and more of his works, written originally in a difficult literary German, have been translated into English.*

One of the most important of these works is Horeb, *presenting the philosophy of Jewish Law as it unfolds from within itself. For Hirsch, this remains the most important element of Judaism, for Torah is not human teaching about God—which is why he disdained the term "Jewish theology"—but God's teaching about and law for man. In* Horeb, *Hirsch presents the 613 Biblical commandments, outlines the broad Halakhic structure they received at the hands of the Rabbis who formulated the ancient tradition, and shows their grand design. He classifies the commandments into six major divisions;* Torot, *or doctrines, the historically revealed ideas concerning God, man, and Israel;* Mishpatim, *or judgments, the laws which lead to the practice of justice toward other human beings;* Hukkim, *the statutes which regulate men's conduct to-*

ward subordinate creatures, whether mineral, vegetable, or animal; Mitzvot, *commandments, the precepts of love toward other human beings;* Edut, *the symbolic observances which, by word or deed, bear lessons for the individual Jew, the people of Israel, or all of mankind; and* Avodah, *service or worship.*

The selection that follows is taken from Mitzvot, *the specific excerpts coming from two chapters, "Setting Up House" and "Kiddushin and Nissuin," the Hebrew names for the two parts of the marriage process.*

> And God blessed them [man and woman],
> and God said unto them, "Be fruitful
> and multiply, and replenish the earth
> and subdue it; and have dominion over the
> fish of the sea and over the fowl of
> the air and over every living thing
> that creeps on the earth."
>
> —GENESIS 1:28

Perpetuate your race. Extend the thread of the generations and raise up descendants to carry on what you have started. Plant in the garden of God new human shoots to whom you will mean everything and whom you will train to serve God. There can be no higher activity than to bring into existence human beings, so that you may train them toward the perfecting of humanity. And there is no greater blessing than to succeed in this endeavor.

In order to do so properly, God says: Make the world the right kind of dwelling place for man. Begin with a family. Form a circle around yourself, and into this circle draw the largest number of God's creatures and gifts in order that you and yours may be able to flourish in it. This circle is the home and the gifts—your property.

It is unfortunate, young man, if you imagine that money and property are enough to make you the true father of a family. Certainly, that will suffice for you to feed and clothe their bodies. But is that all you will need to raise them for God, for Israel, for mankind? Will you be able to nourish the mind and spirit too? Will you be able to transmit to your children the Jewish heritage given to you, and fulfill the claims that God and Israel and humanity make upon you? Are health and manners and skill and worldly wisdom all that they demand of you? Does not your heart tell you that they demand something higher of you?

It is a pity if you are so bewitched by the voice of the age and so little understand your own high mission in life that in amassing material goods you neglect to develop your inner life. Alas for you, and for the hopes pinned on you by your people and by mankind, if you contemptuously abandon the spirit and duty of Israel while you devote yourself exclusively to the pursuit of wealth. Can you possibly bring up aspiring young people to be fully Jewish and human, if you have not completed the process in yourself?

No, young man, this is not the will of your God, this is not the purpose of your mission as man and Jew. Increase your wealth, but before all else gather in the riches of the inner life. Count that day as wasted in which, while you may have added to your financial worth, you have not become richer in the spiritual and ethical treasures of Israel.

Once you have sufficiently enriched yourself spiritually and materially, and you have the means necessary for a family of your own, then and only then look around among the daughters of your people for a wife to bring into your circle. Together with her you may found and sustain a household in which the spirit and word of God is cherished in action and thought.

When you choose a wife, remember that she is to be your companion in life, in building up your home, in the performance of your life task, and choose accordingly. It should not be wealth or physical beauty or brilliance of mind that makes you decide whom to marry. Rather, look for richness of heart, beauty of character, and good sense and intelligence. If, in the end, you require money, and your wife's family freely offers it to you, you may take it; but woe to you and your future household if you are guided only by considerations of money.

Study well the character of your future wife; but since character is first revealed by contact with real life, and since the girl usually first comes into contact with real life only with marriage, look well at her family. If you see a family in which disputes and quarreling are rife, in which insolence and evil talk are common, in which you behold hard-heartedness, hate and uncharitableness, do not attach yourself to it. According to the view of our Sages, even the Jewish descent of such a family is considered doubtful. That you should keep aloof from all marriages forbidden by Torah and the Rabbis goes without saying. Our Sages recommend that one should always look for the daughter of a learned man; of a man in whom the public has shown its confidence by entrusting him with communal office; above all, of a man whose daughter can be expected to have learned practical wisdom from the example of her father. In choosing a wife you have to look for physical no less than for moral and mental soundness, in order that she also may be capable of enduring the hardships and burdens of founding and maintaining a household.

The administration of the household is twofold. The first is the task of the husband. This consists of acquiring as much as possible of material and spiritual assets, of the use of these assets, and of protecting the home and representing it to the outside world. The second is the task of the wife: the wise day-to-day use of what has been acquired, their fair distribution to members of the household, and continually watching over the individual members of the family and training them for their life's tasks.

The founding of a home is the highest task in life because our people and all mankind flower only in and through the home, and because it is there that the younger generation is brought up for God. Because that task is so important, it can be performed only by man and woman together, neither by one nor the other alone. That is why God implanted in the human heart the love of man for woman and of woman for man. Through this love, man and woman unite for the true purpose of life, which neither can execute alone. Together, as the Sages say, they become a "human being" in the full sense of the term. Therefore the man leaves his parental home, attaching himself to a wife, so as to found a family and become a single being; and the wife clings to her husband and willingly subordinates herself to him. Such a union of man and woman for the true purpose of life is called "marriage," and it is of the making of such a marriage that the law speaks.

There are two sides to marriage: one, the union of husband and wife for carrying out the purpose of life; the other the accomplishment of that purpose by means of the home. Corresponding to these two aspects are the two steps by which a marriage is concluded, *kiddushin* and *nissuin*. *Kiddushin*, consecration, signifies the exclusive dedication and transference of the woman to the man; this achieves the personal union of the husband and wife. *Nissuin*, taking to oneself, the reception of the wife into the husband's house, signifies the joint performance of their life task through the home.

Kiddushin: Wherever it is desired to give an object a specific place in human society, this is effected by means of the word. It is the word which expresses the significance that the object shall henceforth bear for mankind. All law is based on notions and the words that express them. Nevertheless, in most cases the fleeting word must be reinforced by some visible action which in its turn embodies and holds the word fast. The word is fixed for all time by such acts as being written down, the transference of a commodity by one person to another, acceptance of payment or some symbol representing the payment, etc.

Here, too, where a human being is to receive a new character, where the woman is to dedicate herself exclusively to the man and the man to the woman, this dedication is accomplished through the word and through an act embodying the word.

The woman belongs exclusively to the man as soon as, in the presence of two competent witnesses, he gives to her the value of a *perutah* (penny) of his property while repeating the words: "You are sanctified to me by this . . . according to the law of Moses and Israel," and she freely accepts what is offered. *Mekuddeshet* ("sanctified") is the precise word which expresses the character of the woman as a wife, as being withdrawn from every other man and belonging only to the one man who regards her as consecrated to him. The man makes the declaration since he, as the sole representative of the household, consecrates her to himself as a wife. The wife now gives herself to him, devoting all her powers to the fulfillment of her life's task within his station and his calling. He gives her a specified portion of his property, symbolizing with it the total product of all his labors, which henceforth belongs to his wife and his family. In return the wife gives herself up wholly to him. She must accept the proffered gift of her own free will, since no consent may be extorted from a person against his will. This procedure must take place in the presence of two witnesses competent to testify. A witness is one who personally perceives an event, retains it in his memory, and so gives permanence to what is transitory. Where human personalities are concerned, only society can be witness. Society, however, is most simply represented by its minimum membership—i.e., not less than two. Such is the supreme importance attached to marriage in the affairs of society that if society is not represented at it by two of its competent members as witnesses, the marriage is void. To be properly qualified, such witnesses must be free men; they must have attained their religious majority; they must be in full possession of their physical and mental faculties; they must belong to the religious union (i.e., not be non-Jews); they must be of unblemished character; they must be entirely outsiders to the affair (i.e., not be related to one of the parties); and they must definitely constitute two sources of evidence (i.e., not be related to one another).

Only through such a union do man and woman become husband and wife. This most holy of human tasks should never be performed casually and without due consideration; otherwise it might appear as utterly unworthy. It should not be consummated without previous courtship, and not in a chance encounter. The bridegroom's gift should be worth at least one *perutah;* usually a ring is used. It must be wholly the property of the bridegroom. No ring with a precious stone should be used, since not everyone knows how to value such a thing. The brides are usually veiled, and they take it for granted that the *kiddushin* ring is worth at least a *perutah.* It is customary to place the ring on the forefinger of the right hand. The witnesses must be present at the whole of the proceedings. The man's declaration must state that he herewith consecrates the woman as his wife, and so it must be understood by her also. Even without any express declaration by the bride, if what has been said already makes it clear that the ring has been accepted and given as being meant for *kiddushin,* it effects the *kiddushin.*

With *kiddushin,* the personal appropriation is completed; the bridegroom is called *arus* and the bride *arusah.* Marriage to anyone else is impossible; the bond can be dissolved only by death or

divorce. Nevertheless, so long as the marriage has not been consummated by *nissuin* and the wife has not therewith been received
into the house of the husband, the consequences do not extend beyond this personal relationship. The husband is not yet her representative, and he has therefore neither the duties of a husband,
such as maintenance, clothing, etc., nor the rights, such as to her
property, service, earnings, inheritance, etc. Still, the *arus* is under
an obligation to take his betrothed into his house within a definite
time and therefore to consummate the marriage with *nissuin.* Before *nissuin,* a "betrothed" couple may not live together in the
same house; the same applies if they are only "engaged."

Nissuin: Marriage is consummated only by *nissuin,* which is related to the Hebrew word for elevation, i.e., reception of the wife
into the house of the husband. This is effected by the simple act of
the *huppah,* or enveloping. A covering which embraces man and
wife together symbolizes visibly the household which they are to
build and which is to embrace their joint activity. By taking the
woman consecrated to him under this covering, the man completes
the marriage by founding a household; henceforth the wife belongs
not only to him but also to his house. Customs differ in regard to
the form taken by the *huppah;* it can be a coverlet supported on
four pillars beneath which the man and woman stand; or the man
envelops both himself and his wife-to-be with the *tallit,* the reminder of the divinely appointed task in life. As soon as the *arusah* has been received under the *huppah* she is called *nessuah,* one
taken into the house, and belongs exclusively to the household of
the husband. All rights and duties arising from the idea of
"house" begin with this moment.

It is customary nowadays (as distinct from Talmudical times) to
perform *kiddushin* and *nissuin* immediately after one another, in
order to avoid prolonging the middle stage of *erusin.*

The woman is highly prized in Israel. She is to be the priestess
of the house. If our Law does not assign to her a part in the public life of the people, it gives her a high position in the home, in
the sphere of her vocation. It demands of the husband deep love,
regard, and respect toward her, and says: only one who loves his
wife as himself and honors her more than himself fulfills his duty
as a husband. The wife should be the holiest possession of the

husband. And he should belong only to her and to his home with every object that he acquires, with every faculty that he possesses, with every joy that comes to him, with his whole being. The husband should see in his wife the being who perfects his manhood, the great central pillar of his household, the better part of himself. He should love her as such and honor her and remain true to her, as the creator of her life's joys, as her masculine support in life's journey, her shield, protection, and strength. Alas for them if it is not so, if man and wife drink only once from the same cup of life —namely, at the time of marriage—and thereafter, while they remain outwardly united, their hearts and lives drift apart. Alas for them if the wife has to bewail the brutality and neglect of the husband. Alas for them if the angel of peace and intimacy flees away, and the consuming fire of discord remains. Only warm mutual love, concern, and fidelity bring to completion what *kiddushin* have begun. Only joint love and fear of God and trust in God complete the work of *huppah*. Such is Jewish marriage, such the Jewish household.

9. Marital Sex

The problem of sexual morality is nothing new, although the "sexual revolution" of our times has given it a new urgency. Judaism has dealt with it from the very beginning. But Judaism's values in the realm of sex must be seen in the larger context of its views on human personality formed in the image of God. Its attitude toward relations between man and woman usually reflects, and often determines, its major thinking on other, apparently unrelated problems.

The Torah warned Israel against the immoral abominations of the Egyptians, from whose civilization it had just emerged, and the Canaanites, whose land it was shortly to enter (Leviticus 18:3). Sex law became a major branch of Judaism, with the Sages' legislation concerning not only illicit relationships—such as adultery and incest—but also the ongoing relationships between husband and wife. In this way the Torah links the most intimate areas of life to religious value: all of life is thus replete with opportunities for behavior based on religious precepts.

Generally, we find Judaism taking the middle road between paganism and Christianity in its assessment of sexuality. Pagans were usually permissive and their rites sometimes obscene, by Jewish standards. Christianity, in its classical form, reacted against this libertinism with a tightening of the rules and a decidedly ascetic, antisexual orientation. Judaism fundamentally acknowledged human sexuality, but carefully controlled its expression in acknowledgment of its potential excesses and dangers.

This is not to say, however, that all pagans were cast in the same mold or that there was total uniformity of views among early Christians. Even in classical Judaism one can find varying interpretations.

Interestingly enough, the more philosophical and rationalistic Jewish thinkers tended toward a negative view of sexuality. Maimonides, for example, considered touching obscene, whereas some in the Kabbalistic tradition held views which appear remarkably "modern" in their natural acceptance of sexuality as part of human physiology and psychology.

One such mystic is the thirteenth-century author of *Iggeret Hakodesh* ("The Letter on Holiness"), a monograph on conjugal relations. For a long time the work had been attributed to the great Nahmanides (R. Moses ben Nahman). Contemporary scholars have demonstrated, however, that Nahmanides could not have been the author. Some identify the author as R. Joseph Gikatilla, while others maintain he was R. Azriel of Gerona—both were thirteenth-century Spanish-Jewish mystics.

🌿

SEX
FROM: THE LETTER ON HOLINESS
Attributed to Nahmanides

A major theme of this remarkable little book is the subsequent effect of the thoughts of the couple on any child conceived during coitus. If husband and wife entertain exalted ideas at such a time, if their approach to each other is tender and refined, the children will be good and noble and will follow in their parents' footsteps. If parents are vulgar and coarse, the children will be alienated from them. The modern reader will decide whether he is ready to accept a direct cause-and-effect relationship between meditation during coitus and the character of the offspring of this union. But certainly there is a large element of truth—moral if not scientific —in the assertion that the manner in which parents treat each other sexually is somehow reflected in the general upbringing of their children.

A second major thrust of this book concerns the essential beauty or at least naturalness of sex—both act and organs. The author is critical of Maimonides and others who ascribed ugliness to sex, and marshals proof from the sources of the Jewish tradition to demonstrate the validity of his approach. What God has made, he teaches, cannot be bad or ugly. Man alone, by misusing the divine gifts, can sully what is pure and noble.

The author apparently intended that the book be read on two levels—one obviously literal, the other a deeper inner mystical one open only to initiates. He saw in marriage a metaphysical symbol of the greatest importance.

Chapter II

Know that union between husband and wife may be considered under two headings:

First: coitus is something holy and clean when it is performed properly, at the proper time, and with the proper intentions. Let no one think that proper coitus is shameful or ugly. Heaven forbid! For the sexual act is referred to as "knowledge" [as in "carnal knowledge"], and for good reason. Thus we read, "and Elkanah knew his wife Hannah" (I Samuel 1:19). The mystical reason for this is that when the act is performed in holiness and purity, the seminal drop derives from the divine sphere of Knowledge and Understanding [two of the three highest of the ten *Sephirot,* whereby God turns to the world, and which pattern also describes man's inner life *]. These are characteristic of the mind. Were there no element of great sanctity connected with the sex act, it would never have been called "knowledge."

Maimonides, of blessed memory, was wrong when, in his *Guide*

* See Introduction to Chapter I on the *Sephirot.*

for the Perplexed (2:33), he praised Aristotle for declaring that the sense of touch is disgraceful for us. Heaven forbid that we say so! We cannot agree with the teaching of that Greek, for this doctrine contains an unsuspected trace of apostasy. It is the result of his [Aristotle's] theory that the world is eternal and uncreated; had he believed that the world was freely created by God, he would never have said what he did. But we, the people of the holy Torah, we believe that the Lord created everything as His wisdom directed, and that He created nothing that was ugly or shameful. Were we to maintain that sex is obscene, we would have to say that the organs of generation are obscene. But this cannot be, for the Lord, may His Name be exalted, created them, as it is said, "Has He not made you and established you?" (Deuteronomy 32:6). And the Sages said in the Talmud (*Hullin* 56b) that God created man so that only in this manner can he perpetuate himself and survive. And the Midrash (to Koheleth 2:12) teaches that God and His heavenly court, as it were, considered each organ of man and had to approve it before creation. Were the sex organs dishonorable, how would the Lord have created anything faulty or blemished or contemptible? Did not Moses say of Him that "the Rock—His work is perfect" (Deuteronomy 32:4)? And did we not learn that "and God saw all that He had made, and behold it was very good" (Genesis 1:31)?

The truth of the matter is, rather, that the blessed Lord is "of eyes too pure to behold evil" (Habakkuk 1:13), and did not make anything defective or shameful. It is He who created man and woman and He created all their organs and prepared them according to their functions, and made nothing disgraceful. The clearest evidence for this is that in the Garden of Eden, Adam and Eve went about undressed and they were not ashamed (Genesis 2:25). All this took place before they sinned, while their minds were fixed on pure thoughts and their intentions were only for the sake of Heaven. Therefore, their sex organs were, for them, no different from eyes or hands or other organs. But when they strayed after physical pleasures and no longer intended their actions for the sake of Heaven, then "they knew they were naked" (Genesis 3:7). This should be understood as meaning that just as hands, when they write the scroll of Torah, are considered honorable and praiseworthy and exalted, but when they steal or otherwise indulge in dishonorable acts are regarded as ugly—so was it with the organs of generation of Adam and Eve: before they sinned it was one way, after they sinned quite different. Just as we ascribe honor and praise to any organ when it serves to do good, and shame and ugliness when it is the instrument of evil, so was it with regard to the first man's sexual apparatus.

Accordingly, the ways of the Lord are all just and pure and clean. What is obscene is the result of man's wrongful actions. This is what Solomon meant when he said, "Behold, this alone have I found, that God made man upright; but they have sought out many devious devices" (Koheleth 7:29). From the point of view of this natural state, the way they were created, there is no defect or ugliness that inheres in any organ of man's body, for all came about through Higher Wisdom as complete and acceptable. But man, because he is a sinner, brings about ugliness where there was none before. Understand this well.

The Rabbis taught us a great secret: when a man has congress with his wife in holiness, the Divine Presence rests with them. If not—it departs from them and they consume each other like two fires. The Sages had this in mind when they taught that there are three partners in the creation of man—father, mother, and the Holy One (*Niddah* 31a). And the Talmud adds that when one honors his parents, the Holy One says, "I consider as if I dwelt with them and he was honoring Me too" (*Kiddushin* 30b). Now, if sex were shameful, how would the Rabbis dare to include God in something that is disgraceful and contemptible? The Torah tells us concerning Abraham and Rebecca and Rachel and Leah and Hannah that God promised to give them children. He promised us that childlessness would not occur in the Holy Land (Exodus 23:26). The Sages taught that one of the three things that, in effect, God tends to personally without delegating it to an angel is pregnancy (*Taanit* 2a). Were all this obscene, why would He do it Himself and not assign it to an angelic messenger?

From all this we may gather that the words of this Greek [Aristotle] are false and invalid, for when coitus is performed for the sake of His Name, there is nothing holier or purer than it. But when people are wicked, the act is impure, and God has no part in it.

So, now that I have told you the first of the two matters concerning conjugal relations, I will try to enlighten you concerning the second matter. And that is the reverse of the first. Namely, when a person engages in the sex act and his intentions are not for the sake of Heaven, the seed that issues from him is considered a "fetid drop," and God has no part in it. About such does the Torah say, as in the story of Noah's generation, "for all flesh had corrupted their way on the earth" (Genesis 6:12). This is the way to the destruction of the body, it is equivalent to offering devotions to an idol, or planting a tree that is worshipped by idolators, for he sows corrupt seed. The offspring of such intercourse become wicked and estranged. But the Torah taught us, "And you shall be holy, for I am holy" (Leviticus 20:26).

Chapter VI

It is well known that a pious and modest person will speak softly, delicately, and pleasantly. He will never talk arrogantly. When he walks, he will do so with head bowed and eyes downward. So will his character express itself in other modes of conduct. The wicked man is just the opposite.

Now, if you are intelligent you will understand that in matters which people do not consider inherently ugly, they can by their actions make them so; certainly with regard to sex, which most people consider inherently shameful. Here, certainly, the pious man must conduct himself with special seriousness.

Therefore, when engaging in relations with your wife, do not conduct yourself frivolously, speaking falsely or vulgarly. Do not be disrespectful toward your wife, and do not engage excessively in trivial and vain talk. Therefore, begin by speaking with her in a manner that will draw her heart to you and calm her spirits and make her happy, so that your minds will be bound up one with the other, and your intention will unite with hers. Speak to her so that some of your words will lead her into desire and love and will and passion; and part of them will attract her to fear of Heaven and piety and modesty. Tell her how pious and modest women were blessed with upright, honorable, and worthy children, students of Torah, God-fearing, and people of accomplishment. . . .

A man should never force himself upon his wife, and never rape her, for the Divine Spirit never rests with one whose conjugal relations are performed in the absence of desire and love and free will. One should never argue with his wife, and certainly never strike her, on account of sexual matters. The Talmud tells us that just as a lion tears apart its prey and eats it shamelessly, so does an ignorant man shamelessly strike and sleep with his wife (*Pesahim* 49b). Rather, act so that you win her heart by wooing her with words of charm and seduction, and other words that are appropriate and worthy, so that both your intentions should be for the sake of Heaven. A man should also not have intercourse with his wife while she is asleep, for then they cannot both agree together to the act. It is far better, as we have said, to arouse her with words that placate her and inspire desire in her.

May God in His mercy open our eyes to the light in His Torah and enable us to perceive the secrets of His Torah and to bring into the world children prepared to revere Him and serve Him. Amen.

10. Children and Parents

In almost all human cultures, it is taken for granted that parents have obligations to provide for their progeny, and children are required to obey their parents. But the acknowledgment of these bare responsibilities tells little about the quality or strength of the family structure created. Jewish law formulates the minimal duties expected of the family members. But for the emotional attitudes and for an indication of the realities of Jewish domestic life as it existed in Talmudic times, as well as for a sense of the Rabbis' ideals of family relations, we must turn to the *Aggadah,* the non-legal Jewish literature.

THE TALMUD
TRACTATE KIDDUSHIN (29a, 30b–31b)

In this Talmudic passage there is no clear and distinct separation between the Halakhic and the Aggadic discourses. Quite typically, they are completely intertwined.

Following the standard Talmudic forms, the passage begins with a Mishnah, a law from the code of R. Judah the Nasi, a body of literature compiled at the end of the second century C.E. *The Mishnah deals with familial obligations, among other things. Its style is brief and concise, though sometimes obscure. In the lengthy Gemara section that follows, the pithy legal terms of the Mishnah are examined, explained, and amplified. The Gemara here (as distinct from that in the smaller, less authoritative Jerusalem Talmud) was composed in Babylon over a period of several hundred years, while the Mishnah was written in Palestine. Yet there is no religious or cultural break between the two. The Gemara is in effect the continuation of the Mishnah. However, the Gemara is different in tone: its method is not systematic like a code; it is, rather, associative, one topic suggesting another, as in a living conversation. In fact, the Gemara is the actual record of the colloquia in the Babylonian academies concerning the Mishnah and its meaning.*

There is also an extraordinary continuity in problem and teaching from Palestine to Babylon to the present generation. The delayed adulthood of youths who spend long years in school and the "generation gap" are not entirely new phenomena. Much of the present difficulty in communications between parents and children represents an intensification of attitudes built into the very nature of human beings. There have always been selfish parents who had to be coerced by the law into providing for their unwanted children. Conversely, there were always overprotective parents who felt they must give the child everything but a sense of reality, and who could not love a child enough to let him go.

The passage that follows stresses the two principles that must regulate a child's duties toward parents: "honor" and "fear," which the Talmud understands in an active, practical sense, rather than as emotional.

MISHNAH. All the obligations of the son upon the father are binding upon men, but women are exempt; but all the obligations of the father upon the son are binding on both men and women. All positive commandments which must be carried out at particular times or seasons apply only to men, but women are exempt; but all positive commandments whose time is not limited are binding upon both men and women. All negative precepts, whether limited to time or not, are binding upon both men and women, excepting: "Do not round the corners of your heads" (Leviticus 19:27); "Do not mar the corner of your beard" (*ibid*.), and "the priest shall not defile himself" for the dead (*ibid.*, 21:1).

GEMARA. What is the meaning of, "All the obligations of the son upon the father"? Shall we say it means all obligations which the son is bound to perform for his father? Are then daughters exempt from such obligations? Certainly not. For it was taught: "Every man, his mother and his father, ye shall fear" (Leviticus 19:3). It says "every man." From this I know only that a man is required to fear his mother and father; whence do I know this is required of a woman? When it is said, "Every man, his mother and his father, *you* shall fear," the plural implies women as well as men.

Said Rav Judah: This is the meaning: "All obligations of the son which lie upon the father" to do to his son, "are binding on men, but women [mothers] are exempt." We have thus learned something in accordance with what our Rabbis taught: The father is bound to circumcise his son, to redeem him [if the son is a first-born], to teach him Torah, to take a wife for him, and to teach him a craft. Some say, to teach him to swim too. R. Judah said: He who does not teach his son a craft teaches him banditry. Can one really think that is banditry? It is as though he taught him banditry for, having no occupation, he must take to theft.

To take a wife for him. Where in the Bible are we taught this? It is written, "Take wives, and beget sons and daughters; and take wives for your sons, and give your daughters to husbands" (Jeremiah 29:6). The obligation to marry off his son is understandable, for its fulfillment rests primarily with him, since one can always find a bride for his son. But with respect to his daughter, how can the obligation to marry her off rest on him? One cannot always obtain a husband for his daughter. This is the meaning: It is her father's obligation to let her be dowered, clothed, and adorned, so that men should eagerly desire her.

To teach him a craft. Where in the Bible are we taught this? Hezekiah said: It is written in Scripture, "See to a livelihood with the wife whom you love" (Ecclesiastes 9:9). If "wife" is meant literally, we may reason that just as the father is bound to take a wife for his son, so is he bound to teach him a craft for a livelihood. However "wife" may here be but a metaphor for Torah. That does not change the teaching. Just as a father is obligated to teach his son Torah, so is he bound to teach him a craft.

And some say, He must teach him to swim in water too. What is the reason for this? His life may depend on it.

R. Judah said: He who does not teach him a craft teaches him banditry. Can you really think that this is "banditry"? But it is as though he taught him banditry. What is the difference between the previous teacher and R. Judah? They differ in the case where he teaches him how to make a living by engaging in commerce. The first teacher, though mentioning a craft, will be satisfied with any means of livelihood, including business. R. Judah's emphasis on a craft shows that he considers commerce too precarious a means of obtaining a livelihood.

But all obligations of the father upon the son, etc. What is meant by *"all obligations of the father upon the son"?* Shall we say it means all precepts which the father is bound to perform for his son? But do women then have the same obligations? Certainly not. Was it not taught: "The father is obliged to circumcise his son and to redeem him"? Only the father can be thus obligated, but not the mother.

Said Rav Judah, this is its meaning: All precepts concerning a father, which a son is obligated to perform for his father, both men and women are bound thereby. We have thus learned something here in accordance with what our Rabbis taught: "Every man, his father and his mother shall you fear" (Leviticus 19:3). It says "every man." From this I know only that a man is required to fear his mother and father; whence do I know it of a woman? When it is said, *"You* shall fear," the plural implies women as well as men. If so, why does Scripture state "every man"? A man possesses the economic means to fulfill this, but a woman does not generally have independent means with which to fulfill this precept. She is under the authority of others, and her husband, say, may render it impossible for her to show due reverence to her parents. R. Idi ben Abin said Rav said: If she is divorced, then obligations toward parents rest upon her just as much as upon her brother.

Our Rabbis taught: Scripture says, "Honor your father and your mother" (Exodus 20:12), and it is also said, "Honor the Lord with your substance" (Proverbs 3:9). Thus Scripture equates the honor due to parents to that due to God. Scripture says, "Every man, his father and his mother shall you fear" (Leviticus 19:3), and it is also said, "Fear the Lord your God and serve Him" (Deuteronomy 6:13); thus Scripture equates the fear of parents with the fear of God. Scripture says, "He that curses his father or his mother shall surely be put to death" (Exodus 21:17), and it is also said, "Whoever curses his God shall bear his sin" (Leviticus 24:15); thus Scripture equates the cursing of parents with the cursing of God. In respect to striking one's parents, it is certainly impossible to equate them, for the Almighty cannot be struck. However, it is logical that parents should be equated with God, for the three of them, God, father, and mother, are partners in him, the son.

Our Rabbis taught: There are three partners in man: the Holy One, blessed be He, the father, and the mother. When a man honors his father and his mother, the Holy One says, "I consider that as meritorious as if I had lived with them and he had honored Me."

It was taught: Rabbi Judah, the Nasi, said: It is revealed and known to Him who brought the world into existence that a son honors his mother more than his father. That is because she sways him by words. Therefore the Holy One mentioned the father before the mother in the commandment to honor one's parents. It is revealed and known to Him who brought the world into existence that a son fears his father more than his mother. That is because he teaches him Torah. Therefore the Holy One mentioned the mother before the father in the commandment to fear one's parents.

A teacher recited before R. Nahman: When a man vexes his father and his mother, the Holy One says, "I did right in not dwelling among them. For had I dwelt among them, they would have vexed Me."

R. Isaac said: A man who sins in secret has, in effect, trampled on the feet of the Shekhinah, the Divine Presence. Does not Scripture say, "Thus says the Lord, the Heaven is My throne, and the earth is My footstool" (Isaiah 66:1)? Now this one acts as if God were not present in the whole earth. R. Joshua ben Levi said: One should not walk four cubits with a haughty bearing, for Scripture says, "The whole earth is full of His glory" (Isaiah 6:3). R. Huna, son of R. Joshua, would not walk four cubits bareheaded, saying, "The Shekhinah is above my head."

A widow's son asked R. Eliezer: If my father orders, "Give me a drink of water," and my mother does likewise, which one takes precedence? "Leave your mother's honor and fulfill the honor due to your father," he replied, "for both you and your mother are bound to obey your father." The same man then went before R. Joshua, asked the same question, and received the same answer. "Rabbi," he then said to him, "what if she is divorced?" "From your red eyes it is obvious to me that you are a widow's son and the question is purely theoretical," he retorted.

Ulla Rabbah once lectured at the entrance to the Nasi's house: What is meant by the verse, "All the kings of the earth shall make admission to You, O Lord, for they have heard the words of Your mouth" (Psalm 138:4). The verse says not "the word of Your mouth," singular, but "the words of Your mouth," plural. Why is that? When the Holy One, blessed be He, proclaimed, "I am the Lord your God," and "You shall have no other gods before Me," the nations of the world said, "He teaches merely for His own honor." As soon as He declared, "Honor your father and your mother," they recanted and admitted the justice of the first commands too. It took several of His utterances to convince them. Raba said: The same idea may be deduced from the following verse: "The beginning of Your word is true" (Psalm 119:160). Surely it cannot mean that the beginning of God's word is true but not the end? Of course not. But from the latter portion of God's declaration it may be seen that the first portion is true.

It was asked of R. Ulla: How far must one go in giving to parents? He replied: Listen to what a certain heathen named Dama, son of Nethinah, did in Ashkelon. The Sages once desired merchandise from him, from which he would make a profit of six hundred thousand gold denarii. But the key was lying under his sleeping father, and he would not trouble him so as to be able to complete the transaction. Rav Judah said in the name of Samuel: R. Eliezer was asked, how far must one go in giving honor to parents? Said he: Listen to what a certain heathen named Dama, son of Nethinah, did in Ashkelon. The Sages sought jewels for the High Priest's ephod at a profit to the heathen of six hundred thousand gold denarii (R. Kahana taught: at a profit of eight hundred thousand). But as the key was lying under his sleeping father's pillow, he would not trouble him to get it. The following year the Holy One, blessed be He, gave him his reward. A completely red heifer was born to him in his herd. The Sages of Israel went to him to buy the rare animal to sacrifice and use its ashes in the Temple purification rites. He said to them, "I know you, that even if I asked you for all the money in the world for it, you would pay me. But I ask of you only the money which I lost through honoring my father." R. Hanina remarked about this: If one who, as a heathen, is not commanded to honor his parents, yet does so, and he is thus rewarded, how much more so will one who is commanded to honor his parents and does so! This is in accord with R. Hanina's teaching: He who is commanded and fulfills the commandment is greater than he who fulfills it though not commanded.

R. Joseph (who was blind) said: Originally I thought that if anyone would tell me that the Halakhah agrees with R. Judah, who ruled that a blind person is exempt from the commandments, I would make a banquet for the Rabbis. For then I thought I had the merit of not being obligated yet fulfilling them. Now, however, I have heard R. Hanina's dictum that he who is commanded and fulfills the command is greater than he who fulfills it though not commanded. Therefore, on the contrary, if anyone should tell me that the Halakhah does not agree with R. Judah, and I am obligated to fulfill the commandments, I would make a banquet for the Rabbis.

When R. Dimi came on a trip from the Land of Israel to Babylonia, he said: Dama, son of Nethinah, was once wearing a gold-embroidered silken cloak and sitting among Roman nobles, when his mother came, tore it off from him, struck him on the head, and spat in his face; yet he did not shame her.

Abimi, son of R. Abbahu, recited: One may give his father pheasants as food and yet deserve banishment from the world. Another may make his father grind in a mill and yet merit the life of the world-to-come. It all depends upon whether the son's attitude is begrudging or consoling.

R. Abbahu said: Anyone who behaves like my son Abimi has fulfilled the precept of honoring. Abimi had five ordained sons in his father's lifetime. Yet whenever his father R. Abbahu came and called out at his door, Abimi himself speedily went and opened it for him, crying, "Yes, yes," until he reached it. One day R. Abbahu asked Abimi, "Give me a drink of water." By the time he brought it R. Abbahu had fallen asleep. So Abimi stayed with him until he awoke. As a reward, while he stood there bent over his father, Abimi succeeded in interpreting the meaning of the psalm "A son of Asaph" (Psalm 79:1), which he had not previously understood thoroughly.

R. Jacob ben Abbahu asked Abaye: "How shall I conduct myself? Whenever I return from the academy, my father pours out a cup of wine for me and my mother dilutes it to the proper taste with water." "Accept it from your mother," Abaye replied, "but not from your father. Since he is a scholar, he may feel affronted that you permit him to do this service for you."

R. Tarfon had a mother for whom, whenever she wished to get into bed, he would bend down to let her ascend by stepping upon him, and when she wished to descend, she stepped down upon him. He went and boasted thereof in the school. Said they to him, "You have not yet reached half the measure of honor due her. Has she then thrown a purse before you into the sea without your insulting her?"

When R. Joseph heard his mother's footsteps, he would say, "I will arise before the approach of the *Shekhinah*."

R. Johanan said: In a way, happy is he who has not seen his parents for it is so difficult to honor them adequately. We should, however, remember that R. Johanan's father died when his mother conceived him, and his mother died when she bore him. [His statement is more self-comfort than teaching.] Abaye was also a double orphan. How can that be, for Abaye often said: "My mother told me. . ."? That was his foster mother.

R. Assi had an aged mother. Said she to him, "I want ornaments." So he made them for her. "I want a husband." "I will look for one for you." "I want a husband as handsome as you." Since she appeared to be mad, he left her and went to the Land of Israel. When he heard that she was following him, he went to R. Johanan and asked him, "May I leave the Land of Israel for abroad?" "It is forbidden," R. Johanan replied. "But what if it is to meet my mother?" "I do not know," said he. R. Assi waited a short time and again came before him. "Assi," said he, "you have determined to go; may the Lord bring you back in peace." Then R. Assi went to R. Elazar and said to him, "Perhaps, God forbid, R. Johanan was angry?" "What did he say to you?" he asked. "The Lord bring you back in peace," was the answer. "Had he been angry," R. Elazar rejoined, "he would not have blessed you." In the meanwhile R. Assi learned that her coffin was coming. "Had I known," he exclaimed, "I would never have left her."

Our Rabbis taught: One must honor one's parents in life, and must honor them in death. "In life" implies that one who is given special attention in a place on account of his father should not say, "Let me go, for my own sake," "Speed me, for my own sake," or "Send me, for my own sake," but all "for my father's sake." "In death," implies that if one is reporting something he heard from his father, he should not say, "Thus did my father say," but "Thus said my father, my teacher, for whose rest may my acts be an atonement." But that is only within twelve months of his death. Thereafter he must say, "His memory be for a blessing, for the life of the world-to-come."

Our Rabbis taught: When a Sage teaches and he wishes to cite a saying of his father, he must not refer to him by name but must refer to him as "my father and teacher." But the "interpreter" [who repeats the Sage's lecture before the scholars at the academy] need not change his father's name and his teacher's name. Whose father? The father of the interpreter? That could not be, for is not the interpreter obliged to honor his own parents? But, said Raba, it means the name of the Sage's father or the name of the Sage's teacher. As when Mar, son of R. Ashi, lectured at academy sessions, he said to the interpreter: "My father, my teacher, said thus." When the interpreter repeated the lecture, he said: "Thus did R. Ashi say."

Our Rabbis taught: What is "fear" (in "every man, his mother and his father shall you *fear*"), and what is "honor" (in *"Honor* your father and your mother")? "Fear" means that the son must neither stand in the father's regular place nor sit in his seat, nor contradict his words, nor side with his father's opponent in dispute when his father is present. "Honor" means that he must provide him with food and drink, clothe and cover him, lead him in and out. The Sages asked: At whose expense? Rav Judah said: The son's. R. Nahman ben Oshaia said: The father's. The Rabbis gave a ruling to R. Jeremiah (others state: to R. Jeremiah's son) in favor of the view that it must be at the father's expense. An objection was raised: Scripture says, "Honor your father and your mother," and it also says, "Honor the Lord with your substance." Just as the latter means at personal cost, so the former too. But those who hold that one must honor the father at the father's expense answer that the son too bears part of the cost, namely, the loss of time from his own work.

11. The Old

The old or elderly have two general claims on society; the satisfaction of those claims is often a measure of the nature of that society. The first is the recognition that, together with all who are weak and infirm, the aged are entitled to society's compassion and assistance. Disease and injury, whether physical or financial, are accidental; the powerlessness that comes from growing old is completely natural and the common lot of almost all who survive to old age.

The second claim is more debatable but equally important: that men owe respect and reverence to the aged on the grounds that years bring with them a certain wisdom which, even if not academic and analytic, is deeply personal and tested in the crucible of experience. Alternatively, the old should be honored if not for wisdom then at least for sheer survival, for having been in God's world longer than most others and for having suffered His judgment and experienced His miracles more extensively than others.

Throughout the ages, Jewish society has taken a positive attitude toward the elder, or *zaken*. The term was first applied in the Bible to Abraham, then to Isaac, Jacob, Joshua, Eli, Samuel, David, and other famous personalities. In formulating its attitude to the old, Judaism considered both claims—that of compassion for the old person as one who is weak, and that of respect for him either as a repository of wisdom or as one whose very age makes him worthy of honor. Indeed, one of the first problems discussed in the passage that follows is how to define the term *zaken,* elder: as primarily a person advanced in years, thus emphasizing his infirmity, as one whose sheer endurance marks him off from others, or as a man of wisdom, which then makes the term *zaken* independent of age.

Careful reading of Jewish sources reveals a moderate, common-sense attitude toward the old rather than indulgence in ancestor-worship. In the passage below, age is not automatically accepted as a guarantee of wisdom, but it is nevertheless commanding of respect. The infirmities of old age, however, are also negative in certain respects. For example, activities requiring a steady hand and a degree of physical stamina are ruled out for the old.

One thing is clear: Judaism does not condone an attitude of neglect of the aged. It does not permit us the illusion that the moral obligation of the young toward the old can be discharged simply by paying a geriatric social worker to keep the old folks occupied. It is equally at odds with an undiscriminating ancestor worship as with the ancient pagan practice of abandoning the elderly on mountain tops to hasten their death—or with the cruelty, both physical and psychological, of the modern institutionalization of the old.

Any society which permits its young to treat their elders with contempt has, for the Talmud, given a sure sign of its social, political, and spiritual disintegration. According to the Rabbis, one of the symptoms of the disastrous age that would usher in the Messiah is just such discourtesy of the young to the old.

BY THE LIGHT OF HALAKHAH
Shelomoh Yosef Zevin

In the following selection, we find a totally unsentimental but compassionate expression of Judaism's concept of the problem of the old in society. The Bible had legislated briefly concerning the zaken. *But how is the term to be defined, how broadly or how narrowly is it to be understood? Furthermore, the Torah commanded us not only to honor the* zaken, *but also to rise in the presence of "the gray head." Are these two terms synonymous, and if not wherein do they differ?*

These are some of the problems taken up by Rabbi Shelomoh Yosef Zevin, one of the most distinguished Talmudic scholars of our generation. A zaken *himself, in both senses of age and profound learning, Rabbi Zevin, a Jerusalemite, is Editor-in-Chief of the renowned* Encyclopedia Talmudit. *In addition to his scholarship and saintliness, Rabbi Zevin has also popularized Halakhah in modern Hebrew as have few others in our generation, thanks to his gifted style. In what is best described as a Halakhic essay, he provides an informative, comprehensive résumé of the entire literature on a specific subject, spanning the whole of Jewish history. His* Le-or Halakhah (By *the Light of the Halakhah), from which this chapter on old age is excerpted, was first published in 1957 and has since been reprinted in several editions.*

The *zaken* or "elder" is considered by Halakhah in three senses: as a scholar and worthy; as an old man; and as one who is weak and infirm. In the first sense of scholar, the term "elder" is merely a metaphor and we shall therefore not deal with it here as such. Rather, we shall concern ourselves primarily with one who is an elder literally, i.e., one who has attained old age. Some laws depend upon actual age itself, and others relate to the frailty attendant upon advanced age.

"You shall rise before the gray head" (Leviticus 19:37) is an explicit commandment of the Torah. Those who compiled the list of the Biblical laws included it as technically one of the 613 commandments of the Torah. The Tannaim [Rabbis of the Mishnah, approximately the first two centuries C.E.] were of several minds concerning the interpretation of this verse. Thus we read:

"You shall rise before the gray head." I might think that this includes even an old man who is an ignoramus. This is not so, for the verse continues with the words, "and you shall honor the presence of the *zaken,* elder"; and "elder" refers exclusively to a wise man, as it is written, "Gather unto me seventy men from among the elders of Israel" (Numbers 11:16—and here "elders" means people of wisdom and ability, not age). R. Yossi, the Galilean, said, "elder" (*zaken*) is only one who has acquired wisdom, as it is written, "The Lord made me (*kanani*) as the beginning of His way" (Proverbs 8:22—a play on the word *kanani,* similar to *zaken*).

Apparently, both statements—the anonymous first opinion of the Sages, and the second by R. Yossi, the Galilean—agree that the Torah does not refer to chronology in its use of the term "elder." However, the Gemara goes on to explain that there is a difference between them—namely, in the case of one who is a wise man but very young. According to the first opinion, that of the Sages, "elder" necessarily includes two elements, age and wisdom. Thus they disqualify an old man who is an ignoramus; by the same token they would exclude the wise man who is young. According to R. Yossi, the Galilean, however, age makes no difference one way or the other. All that counts is wisdom, which is the single and exclusive definition of "elder."

But there is also a third opinion in a *Baraita* cited by the Gemara: "Issi ben Yehudah says, 'You shall rise before the gray head' includes anyone who has attained advanced age [including an ignoramus]." Most but not all authorities hold that Halakhah accepts this third opinion, that of Issi ben Yehudah. Thus Maimonides teaches, "we must stand up before one who is well advanced in years even if he is not a wise man; and a young man who is wise [a scholar] must do so as well. But it is not necessary to rise to full height; it is sufficient to make a gesture which acknowledges him respectfully." What Maimonides means is that a young scholar need not rise to full height before an old ignoramus, and he may merely make a respectful gesture toward him: however, every other person must rise fully before the old man who is unlearned.

What is the law concerning non-Jewish elders? The Gemara records that R. Yohanan would rise before them. He said, "How many adventures have befallen them!" [That is, they have gone through so much, experiencing the Lord's miracles.] Rava did not fully rise before them, but made a respectful gesture toward them. Abaye stretched out his hand for them to lean upon. The *Rishonim* [medieval Halakhists] were divided on the question. Some held that strictly speaking the law does not include non-Jewish elders in the obligation of "rising" and "honoring." Even according to Issi ben Yehudah they are not included in the category of the "gray head." An "old man who is an ignoramus," and whom we must honor, includes either one who is ignorant and wicked or one who is ignorant and unintelligent, but not the Gentiles. The actions of R. Yohanan, Rava, and Abaye [mentioned above] were not performed because the law of "rising" and "honoring" required it, but because of the "ways of peace" [i.e., the Torah requires us to go beyond the letter of the law in matters affecting communal harmony and good human relations]. Other *Rishonim* maintain that Issi ben Yehudah would legally include non-Jews in the category of "the gray head" and "the old man who is an ignoramus." They decide that one ought to rise fully before an Israelite elder, and that one ought at least make a respectful gesture of acknowledgment and extend his hand to a non-Jewish elder. "One must honor an old man, even a non-Jew, by words and by offering his hand for him to lean upon."

The question of priority now arises: what if two people meet, one an old man who is ignorant, and the other a young scholar [i.e., each possessing a different one of the two constituent elements of "elder"]: who precedes whom in the law of "rising" and "honoring"? The problem is discussed in the Gemara, and the decision is: "With regard to learned counsel [literally: "seating"] follow wisdom: with regard to gatherings, follow age." This means that when the problem concerns honors accorded at functions where scholarship is crucial, such as seating judges in the court or scholars in the academy, or any other occasion in which learning of Torah is somehow involved, we give precedence to the young scholar. When it comes to social occasions, such as a wedding, precedence is granted to the old but unlearned man. In both cases there is one condition attached—that the scholar must be truly wise, and the old man truly old. We may summarize the discussions in the Talmud and the various details of the laws, as follows: If we have before us a very great scholar and a very old man, but the old man is not entirely ignorant, then with regard to learned counsel, we honor the scholar first, and with regard to social occasions we prefer the old man. A very great scholar and an elderly man who is not very old—the scholar gets preference in all cases, whether learned counsel or social. A scholar who is not truly great in wisdom and a very old man—the old man comes first even in learned counsel. If both are only moderate in their respective characteristics, the scholar not overly learned and the elderly man not very advanced in age, we give preference to the old man in all cases. However, there are some *Rishonim* who hold that, in this last case, we treat them as we do two people who are equally superlative, the one in wisdom and the other in longevity, and therefore the wise man comes first in learned counsel, the old man in social gatherings.

Does the law requiring us to rise before and honor the elderly include only men, or women as well? The *Sefer Hasidim* [a medieval German work] writes: " 'You shall rise before the gray head,' etc., includes women." But the author of Responsa *Halakhot Ketanot* disagrees. However, in the Azulai commentary to the *Sefer Hasidim,* the following is quoted in the name of *Bet Yehudah:* "It seems obvious that one must rise before a woman as well as before a man."

What is the definition of *ziknah* (old age, the quality of being elderly) such that one must rise before and honor one who possesses it? In the *Ethics of the Fathers,* one of the books of the Mishnah, we read of the different levels of attainment and obligation that refer to various ages, and included in it is the following: "sixty years old for *ziknah,* and seventy years old for 'the gray head.' " The Halakhic writers used this definition with regard to our subject of rising and honoring. Since we are to rise "before the gray head," this means that we are required to stand up in the presence of one who is seventy years old or older. The author of *Minhat Hinnukh,* however, holds that this is a matter of controversy. We previously cited the view of Issi ben Yehudah, according to whom "the gray head" includes any aged person, learned or ignorant. He would then have to interpret the rest of the verse, "and you shall honor the presence of the *zaken,* elder" as referring to the wise man, i.e., "gray head" is based on age, "elder" on intellect. In that case there is only one definition of age, and that is "the gray head" or seventy years old. This would agree with the opinion of the Halakhic writers mentioned above.

However, there is a contrary opinion by an authority of equal stature. Onkelos, the Aramaic translator of the Torah, who was a Tanna like Issi ben Yehudah, renders the passage as: "You shall rise before one who is learned in Torah, and you shall honor the presence of an old man." This is a reversal of the usual interpretation. For Onkelos, "gray head" is exclusively an intellectual term, and *zaken* or "elder" exclusively a chronological term. Now since according to Onkelos the commandment to honor the aged is expressed by the clause containing the word *zaken*, elder, rather than in "the gray head," we must accept the definition of *ziknah* as the proper criterion; and the *Ethics of the Fathers* records sixty as *ziknah*. Hence, when one reaches the age of sixty he is a *zaken* and we are required to rise before and honor him. So we have two opinions: Issi ben Yehudah would establish seventy as the proper age for being honored, and Onkelos sixty. While most authorities accept seventy as the age of honoring, there are some later decisors who take Onkelos' opinion into consideration and recommend that the proper respect be shown to one of sixty as well.

In addition to the respect that must be shown to the elder, there are other areas of the law where the category of *zaken* becomes Halakhically significant. We read in the Mishnah a law concerning the sending of a divorce by messenger from a man to his wife. In order for the divorce to be effective, the husband must be alive at the time the divorce document is handed by the husband's agent to the hand of the woman or her agent. If the husband is deceased by that time, the woman is considered a widow, not a divorcée—and there are many significant differences between the two categories [such as the rights of inheritance, etc.]. Now the Mishnah teaches: "If one brings a *get* [divorce document] to a wife from the husband who is far away, and the husband was old [*zaken*] or sick when the agent left him, the agent may deliver the *get* to the wife because we presume the husband to be alive." We do not, in other words, suspect that the husband may have expired in the interim. The Gemara comments upon this: Rava said, "This law holds true only if the husband has not attained 'the age of strength' [which means, eighty years old]. But if he already is in 'the age of strength' the divorce may not be delivered." Rava's contemporary, Abaye, disagreed, and found support in earlier authority: a *Baraita* teaches that even if the husband was a hundred years old when the agent left him, he may be presumed to be alive. The Gemara records two responses to Abaye's challenge against Rava. First—that Abaye had indeed proved his point against Rava, and thus there is no ceiling beyond which we cannot accept that the husband is alive. Second—once a person has passed a certain age we legally assume that he will live on [hence, the *Baraita* assumes that the one-hundred-year-old husband will continue to live]. This means that a fairly old man is presumed to be living [the Mishnah's law]; a very old man is not presumed to be surviving [Rava's law]; but an extremely old man is presumed to continue living [the *Baraita*'s law]. The decisors are of different opinions as to how we decide Halakhah. R. Isaac Alfasi and Maimonides and others state simply, and without qualification, that we never question a man's continued survival because of age. Apparently they accept the first response of the Gemara, according to which Abaye had successfully refuted Rava. There are thus no gradations in age, and *ziknah* never dislodges the presumption of survival. But a number of other decisors accept the second answer, thus essentially agreeing with Rava, with the added qualification that beyond a certain age we assume continued survival. Thus, according to this latter school, we have three categories of the elderly with regard to the assumption of continued survival: the youngest of the three, the fairly old, is assumed to survive; the next group, the very old, does not benefit from this presumption; the oldest, the extremely old, is assumed to continue in life. The youngest group begins at age seventy [or sixty, depending upon the definition of *zaken,* as discussed above] and goes to age eighty. The next category, where we do not accept the presumption of survival, is from eighty-one to ninety, according to Rashi. Other authorities extend this questionable or dangerous age to one hundred. Thus, the advanced age beyond which we assume that one who has lived so long will continue to live longer, begins at ninety according to Rashi, and at one hundred according to the other authorities.

"Old or sick" is the way the Mishnah began the discussion—in either case, we assume the man is alive. What, however, if he was both old *and* sick? The author of *Tiferet Yaakov* maintains that even if one were both old and sick he must be presumed to be alive. However, he distinguishes between two kinds of illness. If the sickness was the result of some external injury or disease, unconnected with his age, the husband is to be considered as alive; he is no worse than one who is old *or* sick. However, if his illness was geriatric, the weakness characteristic of advanced age, we no longer may assume his survival.

Thus far we have discussed the definition of "old" or "elderly" as chronological. However, there are those who offer physical symptoms rather than numbers of years as the definition of *ziknah.* Thus: "The Rabbis taught that a *kohen* [priest] is qualified to minister [in the Temple in Jerusalem] from the time of his puberty until he becomes a *zaken.*" The Gemara then asks for the definition of *zaken,* or old man. The answer given is, "until he begins to tremble," i.e., when his hands or feet began to tremble because of the infirmity of old age. This does not imply a merely factual statement that when the *kohen* was too weak to minister he usually no longer continued to perform his duties, but that the law officially disqualifies him on account of *ziknah.*

The question of palsy that comes of old age is relevant to modern Halakhic issues as well. There is a considerable literature in more recent times concerning the *shohet* [ritual slaughterer] whose hands tremble: does this disqualify him from performing his duties [so that if he continued to slaughter under such conditions, the animal would be declared non-kosher]? At first blush, there should be no problem and we should unhesitatingly declare the *shohet* unfit, whether the tremors are the result of illness or age. However, the author of Responsa *Ramatz* maintains that there is a significant difference between them. When the *shohet* develops the palsy because of some external factor such as an illness, we may believe him when he tells us that he does not do any slaughtering during the particular time that he is afflicted, but confines his work to his healthy periods. But when a man develops palsy because of old age, such that the tremors occur at unexpected and unpredictable intervals, he does not have such credibility, and we disqualify him permanently.

However, there are those who prefer the chronological definition of *ziknah* for a *shohet*. Thus, the author of Responsa *Bet Yaakov* forbids anyone over eighty to be a *shohet*. Others are more stringent and maintain that in our generations one over seventy should already cease functioning in this capacity. Most authorities, however, prefer to judge each case on its individual merits: we must determine each person's qualifications according to his own strength and state of health.

In addition to various physical symptoms of aging, there are also psychological criteria discussed in Halakhah. One of these concerns an aging woman. For certain Halakhic reasons it is necessary to determine exactly when a woman becomes a *zekenah* [old woman]. The *Shulhan Arukh,* following a passage in the Talmud, defines a *zekenah* as one who does not mind if she is called [by people outside her own family] "Mother" [the equivalent of "Grandma" used affectionately for any elderly lady]. The Jerusalem Talmud, however, asks: Can we then allow a legal definition to rest with her own feelings, i.e., is this not too subjective a criterion? The Jerusalem Talmud answers that the standard is one who is of such an age that she is *capable* of being called "Mother" without reacting negatively, i.e., other women her age are addressed in this manner without taking offense. We consider the general age group, not the individual's personal reactions. Yet, at bottom, the definition of the *zekenah* does depend upon the inner feelings of the woman—her own resentment [or lack of it], or the resentment or non-resentment of others in the same age group, at being regarded as old. There is yet a further, subtle distinction we find expressed by the *Amoraim* [Rabbis of the Gemara, the period following the Tannaim of the Mishnah]. One Amora defined the *zekenah* as one who is called "Mother" and does not *mind* it; the other—that she is not *embarrassed* by it. The difference arises in the case of a woman who, when addressed in this way, is embarrassed or ashamed [an inner reaction], but does not resent or take offense at it [verbally]. R. Solomon Kluger thus categorizes the types as follows: There is a *zekenah* of advanced age such that she is not even inwardly embarrassed by the appellation "Mother." The youngest category of *zekenah* is one who not only is embarrassed but is explicitly resentful at being called "Mother." The middle category is one who is embarrassed by it, but will not openly express her resentment. [According to the Jerusalem Talmud, these three categories should be defined as *capable* of such reactions, determined by other women of the same age, rather than the individuals reacting in this specific manner.]

The *zaken* may suffer a diminution of his reproductive capacity, but that is not sufficient to warrant violating the law against castration or sterilization. Halakhah prohibits castrating even an older person past the childbearing age because it is sometimes possible to regain the capacity to reproduce by medical treatment. In this respect there is a difference between men and women. The majority of the Sages hold that the first commandment of the Torah, "be fruitful and multiply," applies only to men, who are thus expected to take the initiative in raising a family; women are not under a technical obligation to do so. R. Yohanan ben Berokah holds that women too are commanded to give birth to children. Now according to R. Yohanan ben Berokah, since women are not exempt from the law to reproduce, it is forbidden to sterilize a woman. Nevertheless, he holds that a *zekenah* past the childbearing age may submit to sterilization, whereas an old man in the same category would be forbidden to do so.

Should an old man [re]marry? Halakhah encourages it. "If he married when he was young, he ought to marry when he is old." But this holds true only if he marries someone in his own age group. The Lord will not forgive a man who gives his daughter in marriage to an old man. The *Shulhan Arukh* declares: "A young man should not marry an old woman, and an old man should not marry a young girl; for such mismatching leads to immorality."

The changes in character that come with age are discussed in the Talmud. Thus: it is in the nature of the *zaken* that he is tender and compassionate. So do we find in the Aggadah, which speaks of the variety of ways in which God appears to man: "He revealed Himself on the Red Sea as a hero and a warrior, and He revealed Himself at Sinai as an old man full of compassion." Interestingly, Halakhah takes the opposite view and considers the old man as more prone to cruelty. The Talmud states, "We do not seat as a judge in the Sanhedrin [the Supreme Court] an old man or a eunuch or one who is childless." Rashi explains that all three are rejected as judges because of inadequate tenderness. "An old man is excluded because he has already forgotten the pain and anxiety of raising children, and therefore is no longer compassionate." And Maimonides: "We do not appoint to the Sanhedrin an old man well advanced in years, or a eunuch, because they tend toward heartlessness." But note that Maimonides adds: "well advanced in years." It is not enough that he be "old," but he must be *very* old in order to be disqualified from a seat on the Sanhedrin. This is so because, quite to the contrary, we find that old age is a recommendation for membership in the Sanhedrin. Thus, in a famous passage in the Talmud [found as well in the Passover Haggadah], R. Elazar ben Azaryah says, "Behold I am as one of seventy years. . . ." And the Talmud explains: "as one," but not really seventy years old. For R. Elazar ben Azaryah was a young man when he was elected to head the Sanhedrin, and on that day a miracle occurred and his hair turned white so that he might appear like an old man of seventy. Hence, age not only does not disqualify one for a seat on the Sanhedrin but it is desirable. Furthermore, Maimonides writes that "we must make a special effort to search for members who are all of the age of the gray head." Hence, it would seem from Maimonides that elders are desirable in the Sanhedrin, but not if they are superannuated; for then, having lost contact with family and general community, they lost the capacity for compassion.

What, however, if one entered the Sanhedrin when he was younger, but then in the course of years he reached the age of disqualification: must he resign? Or is the age limit only for newcomers, not for those already on the bench? The question was asked of Rashba [R. Solomon ben Aderet, an eminent Spanish medieval Halakhist]. He inclines toward mandatory resignation because the reason of "heartlessness" is operative.

At the same time, we find support for the opposite view—that which praises the old man for possessing "a broken heart," i.e., a sense of commiseration and compassion. In describing the special prayers recited publicly on the fast days, we are told that the *zaken* of the community would preach warmly, and that a *zaken* experienced in prayer would lead the congregation in their services. Here *zaken* clearly is chronological: a man who is old in years, provided he possesses the other qualifications required of those who lead the congregation in prayer. The special virtue of the old man, in this context, is that, in the words of one of the *Rishonim,* "he is broken of heart, and the seething passions of youth have left him."

12. Sickness and Death

Aman's ethical and spiritual achievements come to the fore most visibly in his approach to death and to those who have been seared by it. The integrity of one's whole view of life is at stake at such times.

That is a reasonable test of a people as well. Its views of life and death are usually expressed in its song, poetry, and stories. The institutionalization of its attitudes in the forms of laws and ritual practices provides an even more significant insight. This gives more than legal interest to the four-hundred-year-old classic code of Jewish Law, the *Shulhan Arukh* [The Prepared Table] by R. Joseph Caro of Safed (1488–1575).

The texts that follow, excerpted from the *Yoreh Deyah,* one of the four great divisions of the code, contain explicit directives for visiting the sick and the dying, the conduct of the physician, and for those who come to console mourners. This is a code for the deportment of those who stand secure and confident at the core of life and society vis-à-vis those who are on the way out, who slip or are pushed beyond the rim, weak, helpless, and in despair.

SHULHAN ARUKH
Joseph Caro

The Shulhan Arukh *deals not with philosophy or theology but with specific acts of behavior, with the particularities of prescribed and proscribed conduct in concrete human situations. It offers these Halakhot, or rules, without explicit reference to any fundamental meaning underlying them.*

Yet there is a substantial philosophy of life and social responsibility implicit in this guide to conduct. Judaism traditionally does not begin with the formulation of a philosophy and on that basis proceed to decide upon consequent modes of action. Jews presuppose that the world-view of Judaism, from Sinai through Talmud, is worthy of assent, whether one knows that view consciously or not, whether one understands it intellectually or not. The primary Jewish task is to obey God by practicing the commandments. The attitudes that inform them will thereby eventually and inevitably become one's own. By living and studying the Halakhah, one gradually discovers and absorbs the theological and moral sources upon which it is based. The method is inductive rather than deductive.

In trying to abstract the Jewish attitude to life from the Halakhot dealing with our responsibility to the sick and the dying and the mourning, however, we must beware of reading too much either into or out of individual laws. We must keep in mind that Caro only compiled the Shulhan Arukh; *he did not originate its contents. In almost every instance, this master of Jewish jurisprudence was confronted with a maze of conflicting opinions on legal details, and he decided each case on its own merits and in accordance with the methods of Halakhic decision-making. It is therefore vain to hope for total consistency of philosophical views to emerge from these laws, or to focus on one or two individual laws and pretend to discover in them more than they really contain or suggest. Furthermore, Caro's* Shulhan Arukh *represents the legal consensus of Sephardi Jewry, while the Notes (called* Mapah, *or*

Tablecloth) *by R. Moses Isserles of Cracow, Poland, embody the somewhat differing legal traditions and folk practices of Ashkenazi Jewry. Modern Jewish practice, determined by the later decisors [posekim], has for the most part been eclectic, sometimes favoring one, sometimes the other.*

Yet there are certain large patterns that emerge from the general trend of the Halakhah. Insistence upon the minutiae of the law, for example, succeeds in forcing us to deal, with effective compassion, with those threatened by life's end and with the bereaved. The normal human reaction might be to turn away from sickness and death, to recoil from contemplating those conditions, to give way to inchoate fears, inner panic, and resultant clumsiness in approaching the dying and the dead.

Chapter 335 contains the idea of the Divine Presence [Shekhinah] resting above the patient. But this is not said in connection with pity for the ill, but rather with a show of respect. The patient, who at least inwardly must face the possibility of his own end, who in his infirmity experiences a sense of social impotence as he is cast out of the streams of business and social intercourse and plucked out of the normal patterns of daily living, who feels reduced to an "it" as he is examined and poked and pushed and pricked and x-rayed—this patient does not need pity but respect so that he may retain his dignity even on the sickbed. That dignity requires that he be told the truth, but without morbidity. Prayer for him includes him in the community of the ill as a reminder that he is not alone in his misery.

The patient is urged to confess his sins and relieve his guilt, but is warned not to misinterpret viduy *[confession] as the certain end.*

Chapter 335: When to Visit the Sick; Which Sick Persons Should Be Visited: How to Pray for the Sick

1. It is a religious duty to visit the sick. Relatives and close friends may visit at once. Strangers should not visit until after three days, lest the patient be prompted to exaggerate his condi-

tion because of the unexpected company of strangers so soon. If the sickness overtakes him suddenly, both categories of visitor may enter immediately.

2. Even a prominent person must visit a humble one, even many times a day. The more one visits the sick, the more praiseworthy is it, provided it is not overdone so that it imposes a burden upon the patient.

NOTE: Some say that one may visit a sick person who is his enemy. However, this does not seem plausible to me; rather, he should not visit a sick person or comfort a mourner whom he hates, so that the latter should not think that he rejoices at his misfortune, and thereby feel depressed. This seems to me to be the correct view, depending upon the individual circumstances.

3. One who visits the sick may neither sit upon a bed, nor upon a chair, nor upon a stool, but must act reverently and sit on the ground in front of the invalid, for the Divine Presence [*Shekhinah*] rests above a sick person.

NOTE: This applies only if the sick person lies on the ground, so that he who sits near him will be on a higher level; but when the patient lies upon the bed, it is permissible for the visitor to sit on a chair or a stool, as long as the visitor is not on a higher level. This is our accepted practice.

4. One ought not visit the sick during the first three hours of the day—for the patient's discomfort is usually alleviated in the morning, and consequently the visitor will not feel constrained to pray for him; and not during the last three hours of the day—for then his illness grows worse and the visitor may despair and thus fail to pray for him.

NOTE: One who visited a sick person and did not pray for him has not fulfilled the religious duty of visiting the sick.

5. In praying for a sick man—if in the presence of the patient, one may pray in any language; if not in his presence, one should pray in Hebrew.

6. In praying for the sick, one should include him in his petition together with other sick of Israel by saying, "May the Omnipresent have compassion upon you in the midst of the sick of Israel," since the merit of an entire group is greater than that of an individual. On the Sabbath, when prayers of petition are inappro-

priate, the visitor says, "It is the Sabbath, when one ought not cry out, but healing will come soon."

7. The patient should be advised to arrange his worldly affairs, and keep a record of what he lent to or deposited with others, or vice versa, and should be asked whether he wishes to leave instructions for his children. He should be told that there is no reason to fear death on account of this.

8. One must not visit those suffering with diseases such that a visit causes the patient either embarrassment or discomfort. Likewise, one who is seriously sick, such that conversation is injurious to him, must not be visited personally, but one may enter the outer chamber and inquire concerning his condition and offer any household or nursing help, and also sympathize with and pray for him.

9. One must visit the sick of the Gentiles, for this contributes to the peace and well-being of society.

10. In the case of those suffering from bowel diseases, a man must not attend upon a woman for reasons of modesty, but a woman may attend upon a man.

NOTE: Some say that whoever has a sick person in his family should go to the Sage of the city in order that he pray for him; and likewise is it the accepted practice to recite blessings on behalf of sick persons in the synagogues when the Torah is read; also to give them an additional name, for a change of name, symbolizing a new identity, causes the evil decree passed upon a man to be canceled. The precept of comforting mourners takes precedence over visiting the sick, since the precepts of comforting mourners is a charitable act on behalf of both the living and the dead.

Chapter 336: Laws of the Physician

This chapter deals with physicians and informs us of their need to be permitted to practice their healing arts. It makes a distinction between law and morality (in the sense of enforceability) in the case of the physician's liability for malpractice.

1. Although the practice of medicine might be considered an interference with the divine decree, nevertheless the Torah (Exodus 21:19) grants the physician permission to heal. Furthermore, healing is considered a religious duty, for it comes under the rule of saving a life. If a physician withholds treatment, he is regarded as a murderer, even if there is someone else who can heal a patient, for it may be that it is the special merit of this physician to provide healing for this specific patient. However, one should not practice medicine unless he is an expert and there is no one immediately available more competent than he; otherwise, he too is regarded as a murderer. If one administered medical treatment without the permission of the Jewish Court, or nowadays without a medical diploma, he is subject to payment of indemnities, even if he is an expert. If he was properly licensed to practice medicine but he erred in his treatment because of negligence, thereby causing injury to the patient, he is exempt by the laws of man, and is held responsible by the laws of Heaven, i.e., he is regarded as morally but not legally responsible. If the physician caused the death of his patient as a result of negligence, he is banished according to the laws relating to one who killed another inadvertently.

2. The physician may not accept a fee for giving advice to the patient, for in imparting of his wisdom and learning to his fellow man he performs the religious duty of restoring health to one who has lost it, and just as the Creator teaches gratis, so must man. However, he may accept payment for the time he spends in visiting the patient and for the trouble he takes to write the prescription.

3. A pharmacist may not raise the price of his medicines above the standard price in order to take advantage of his neighbor's special needs. Furthermore, even if he and his customer agreed to the excessive amount because of the emergency condition—for only he possessed the necessary medical ingredients—the pharmacist is entitled only to the standard price. However, if one stipulated an excessive sum as payment to a physician, he is obligated to give it to him, for the physician sold him his learning, which cannot be valued in terms of money.

NOTE: This holds true even though the physician is obligated as a religious duty to heal him—for every positive command devolves equally upon every person. However, if one chances upon the opportunity to perform this religious duty, and he agrees to execute it only for compensation, the money cannot be recovered from him if it was already paid, and we do not make him cancel his fee if it was not yet paid.

Chapter 337: One Who Is Sick and Suffered a Bereavement

1. One who is sick and who suffered the death of a close relative must not be informed of his bereavement lest he become excessively agitated; nor is his garment rent as is normally required of the mourner; nor is it permitted to cry or lament for the dead in his presence, so that his heart not be broken by fearing his own death as a result of his illness; and, if he is aware of his bereavement, those who come to offer condolences should be told not to dwell on the subject and increase his sorrow.

Chapter 339: Laws Concerning a Dying Man: (Recital of Tzidduk Ha-din)

This chapter reveals two major ideas. The first concerns reverence for life: we may do nothing to hasten death. But does this mean that we must necessarily prolong life beyond endurance? The second concerns the prayer acknowledging divine justice (the Tzidduk Ha-din). Is this an instance of resignation to cruel and blind fate, or is it perhaps a more spiritually valid act of submission to the inscrutability of divine wisdom, whose benevolence remains hidden from man because of his natural limitations? Compare the NOTE *to 376:2.*

1. A patient who is dying is considered a living person in all respects. We may not tie his jaws, anoint him, wash him, plug his open organs, remove the pillow from under him, place him on

sand or clay ground or earth, or perform any other such practices normally done to a corpse. Thus, too, we may not publicly announce his death by summoning mourners and friends to the funeral, nor may we arrange for the funeral before his death. It is forbidden to close his eyes before his soul departs, thereby hastening his death. One who does so is considered a murderer. One may not rend garments in grief as is done after a relative dies, nor make a lamentation or eulogy for him, nor bring a coffin into the house in his presence in anticipation of his death, nor may we begin the recital of *Tzidduk Ha-din,* the prayer to be spoken after death, before his soul departs.

NOTE: Some say that we may not dig a grave for him before he dies. It is forbidden to hasten the death of a dying man, e.g., if one has been moribund for a long time, and continues to linger on, we may not remove the pillow or the mattress from under him in the belief that [according to some] the feathers contained therein prevent him from dying easily; for in the process of touching the patient we may move him and thus hasten his death. He may likewise not be moved from his place. For the same reason, it is forbidden to do anything overt in order to ease his death. However, if there is anything external which prevents his release from his death pangs, such as a clattering noise near the patient's house, or if there is salt on his tongue, and these hinder the departure of the soul, it is permitted to remove them, because here there is no direct act of hastening death, for one merely removes the impediment. However, some authorities forbid removing salt from his tongue, since in this case too the patient has to be moved.

2. One who is informed "We saw your relative in a dying condition three days ago," is required to mourn for him.

NOTE: For it is presumed that he has already died.

3. *Tzidduk Ha-din* [the acknowledgment of divine justice] is recited when the soul departs. When the mourner reaches the words, "Judge of Truth," he rends his garments.

[Nowadays this is recited at the burial service.] Following are excerpts from the *Tzidduk Ha-din.*

What God does is right, for all His ways are just; God of faithfulness and without wrong, just and right is He. Who can say to Him: "What are You doing?" He rules below and above; He causes death and life; He brings down to the grave and raises up again. O You who decree and perform, show us unmerited kindness; for the sake of Isaac, who was bound like a lamb, listen and take action.

You who are righteous in all Your ways, You who are the perfect God, slow to anger and full of mercy—have pity on parents and children; for Yours, O Lord, is forgiveness and mercy.

Just are You, O Lord, in causing death and life; You in whose hand all living beings are kept, far be it from You to erase us from memory; for Yours, O Lord, is mercy and forgiveness.

Whether one lives a year or a thousand years—what does he gain? He is as though he never existed. Blessed be the true Judge, who causes death and life.

We know, O Lord, that Your judgment is just; You are right when You speak, and justified when You give sentence; one must not find fault with Your manner of judging. You are righteous, O Lord, and Your judgment is right.

The life of every living being is in Your hand; Your right hand is full of righteousness. Have mercy on the remnant of Your own flock and say to the angel: "Stay your hand."

We proclaim that the Lord is just. He is my stronghold, and there is no wrong in Him. The Lord gave and the Lord has taken away; blessed be the Name of the Lord.

4. With the approach of death, those who attend the patient should not leave him, lest his soul depart while he is alone.

NOTE: It is a religious duty to stand by a person during the departure of his soul, as it is written, "That he should yet live forever; that he should not see the pit. For he sees that wise men die, the fool and the brutish together perish," etc. (Psalm 49:10).

Chapter 376: The Deportment of the Comforters at the House of Mourning and the Law of a Dead Person Who Leaves No Mourners to Be Consoled by Comforters

This chapter deals with our responsibility to those who die without survivors; the relative significance of reciting the mourner's

Kaddish and leading the public service; the custom (still practiced today) of the mourner's reciting the Kaddish for eleven months instead of a full year.

1. The comforters are not permitted to speak until the mourner initiates the conversation. At meals served in the house of mourning, the mourner takes his place at the head of the table. When the mourner nods his head, indicating that he dismisses the comforters [for it is not permitted for mourner and comforter to exchange greetings either upon meeting or leaving], they are not permitted to remain with him any longer.

NOTE: A mourner or a sick person is not required to rise in honor of any distinguished visitor, even if he be the leader of all Israel.

2. Normally, when one rises as a gesture of respect before an elderly or distinguished person, the latter may say to the former, "Be seated." However, he should not say this if the former is a mourner or a sick person who rose, although he is not required to do so—for such a statement would imply, "Be seated [i.e., remain] in your mourning or illness."

NOTE: A man should not say, "I was not sufficiently punished in accordance with my evil deeds," or anything similar to these words, for a man should never utter anything as if to invite more punishment. Neither should a man say to a mourner, "What could you have done? It is impossible to change God's verdict," for this is regarded as blasphemy, since it implies that were it possible to change the verdict he would have done so; one should rather accept God's decree out of love.

3. If one dies and leaves no mourners, ten worthy people should assemble and stay in the home of the deceased throughout the seven days of mourning [although it is not necessary for them to remain there all day], and the rest of the people assemble unto them [as if they were comforting mourners for the deceased]. If ten people were not available on a regular basis to be present there daily, any ten people assemble in the home.

NOTE: However, I have not seen this custom in practice. In the writings of MaHaRil [Jacob Halevi of Molin, 1365–1427] it is stated that it is customary to conduct services attended by ten males throughout the seven days of mourning in the home of a person who left no known near-of-kin to observe the period of mourning for him; but if there are mourners somewhere who observe the mourning for him, there is no need to do this. This is the proper practice.

4. Nowadays it is customary that after the filling of the grave with earth has been completed [or after the mourners have left the deceased] the mourners remove their shoes and sandals, and move away a short distance from the burial grounds, and then say Kaddish, "May His great Name be magnified and sanctified in the world that He will create anew," etc. After this they pick up some earth, an allusion to human origin and end, and pluck grass, an allusion to the resurrection of the dead, and cast them behind their backs. Upon returning from the funeral, they wash their hands with water.

NOTE: Some say that after the burial, the mourners halt seven times as a symbol of ridding themselves of the spirit of death. In these countries (i.e., Poland, and other Ashkenazi Jewish communities) the custom is to do so only three times, and to do so after they have washed their hands. Each time they halt they say, "And let the graciousness of the Lord our God be upon us," etc. (Psalm 90:17), and "O You that dwell in the shadow of the most High," etc. (Psalm 91). These three stops are performed not only on weekdays, but also on Sabbaths or festivals. After the burial, it is customary not to enter a house before washing the hands and sitting down three times; and the custom of the past is considered law. The Midrash teaches that one should recite Kaddish for a deceased father. It is therefore accepted practice to recite the Kaddish at the end of every service for a deceased father or mother, for a period of twelve months. However, it is the accepted custom to recite the Kaddish for only eleven months, for the punishment of a wicked person is considered as lasting twelve months, and one should not assume this of his parents. While one may not recite the mourner's Kaddish if both his parents are alive, he may recite it for a deceased mother even while his father is living, and the latter has no right to protest. It is a religious duty to fast on the anniversary of the death of a parent. It is customary that on that day one recites the mourner's Kaddish for them. One who knows how to lead the entire service should do so. The mourner's Kaddish is recited only for a parent, not for other close relatives. But there are places where the Kaddish is recited for relatives other than parents. In this matter Jews follow whatever is the established custom of the city. If there is no one present in the synagogue who is in mourning for a parent, the Kaddish may be recited by one who has no father or mother, on behalf of all the dead of Israel. Mourners recite the Kaddish even on Sabbaths and festivals, but it is not customary for them to conduct the service on these days, although there is no prohibition against this. It is customary for the mourner to read the Haftorah [the weekly selection from the Prophets] and to lead the services at the evening prayers at the conclusion of the Sabbath, which is the time when the souls of the departed return to Gehenna after a day of respite; for when the son leads the service and recites the sanctification of the Divine Name in public, he redeems the souls of his parents from Gehenna. During weekdays, however, one who knows how to conduct the service should do so; this is preferable to reciting the mourner's Kaddish, which was originally instituted only for recitation by minors. Although children of an apostate Jew do not recite the Kaddish for him, nevertheless some say that if he was murdered by heathen, his sins are forgiven and hence his survivors do recite the Kaddish.

Chapter 378: The Laws of the Mourner's Meal

This chapter reveals Judaism's moral concern for the mourner isolated in his grief, cut off from social intercourse by his suffering, despising human contact, perhaps even welcoming death for himself as a way out of unbearable misery and some primitive, undefined guilt. The neighbors of the mourner are Halakhically bound to reintegrate him into society, to rehabilitate him personally, to express to him their manifest concern for his elementary needs and welfare. And the mourner is commanded to help in the process by opening himself to the helping hand and heart of his fellow man.

1. A mourner is forbidden to eat of his own food at the first meal upon return from the burial. [The Sages considered it the obligation of the mourner's neighbors to supply that meal for him, even as the Lord told Ezekiel, "Do not eat the bread of man" (Ezekiel 24:17). Some explain that sometimes the mourner refuses to eat and prefers death; the meal provided by the neighbors is thus an act of assisting the bereaved toward his rehabilitation.] If others fail to provide him with this meal, he may eat of his own food. He is permitted to eat his own food for the second meal, even though it occurs during the first day of mourning. One may provide food for another person during the latter's mourning, and the latter may reciprocate during the former's bereavement, provided that they did not arrange to do so in advance.

2. If a woman is in mourning, the mourner's meal should be given to her by other women rather than by men. If a married woman is in mourning, she may not eat the first meal from her own home [that of her husband], for that is considered her own food, since it is incumbent upon her husband to support her. So a scribe or hired man who receives his meals as payment should not eat of his employer's food for his first meal of mourning. But a poor man or orphan who receives his meals from one who gives them as the fulfillment of a religious precept may continue to eat such meals as the first one after burial of a close relative.

3. If the mourner preferred not to eat on the first day, he may eat of his own food for the first meal on the next day. [Some authorities, however, do not permit the mourner to fast because it is a religious duty for the neighbor and the mourner that the meal be eaten.]

NOTE: If he was not provided with the mourner's meal during the first day until nighttime, he is permitted to eat of his own food at night.

4. It was customary to fast on the day of the death of scholars.

5. In the case of one whose relative was buried Friday afternoon close to nightfall, some authorities say that he should be provided then with the mourner's meal. But it seems to me that since this is not obligatory [since it is not right to eat before the advent of the Sabbath], it is better not to provide him with

the mourner's meal then, out of honor for the Sabbath. This is the accepted custom.

6. The mourner's meal is not provided for one who lost an infant child less than thirty complete days old, unless one knows for certain that its mother went through a complete term of pregnancy.

7. One may sweep or mop floors and one may wash dishes and other utensils in the house of mourning, for this is not considered as pleasure. However, one should not spray perfume or bring spices into the house of mourning, although it is permitted to do so in order to fumigate the house where the corpse lay. [In that case one need not recite the usual blessing over spice or incense.] In mourning for a Sage whose academy is in recess, one should not expound the law or offer homiletical interpretations; rather, one sits in silence.

8. After the burial the mourner may eat meat and drink some wine [both prohibited before interment] during the meal, but with moderation.

9. In those places where it is customary to provide the mourner, for his first meal, with meat and wine and savory dishes, this should be done; but first the mourner should be fed eggs or a dish of lentils, symbols of mourning.

10. There should not be too many people to join the mourner in his meal, for if they cannot all fit about one table it may appear more like a social gathering.

11. Where the first day of mourning is postponed, such as when death occurred during the intermediate days of the festival and the week of mourning commences therefore after the end of the festival, the first official mourner's meal should be provided by others.

NOTE: However, some maintain that since the first day of mourning was postponed, there is no need to arrange for the first meal to be provided by others, and this is our accepted practice.

12. In the case of "distant tidings" [i.e., where one observes one hour of mourning upon hearing of the death of a relative that occurred more than thirty days earlier], the mourner's meal is not provided.

13. During the week, the most distinguished among the comforters at the meal breaks bread and recites the blessing thereon. On the Sabbath the mourner himself breaks bread in the usual manner.

PART THREE

Society

13. Business Honesty

Business ethics is a sensitive barometer of morality. While friendships, domestic relations, community leadership all reflect a man's social conscience, money remains a key to discovering the nature of a man as a social being. Land can be measured, money can be counted, goods can be weighed—and a man knows soon enough whether he is going to accept a loss for the sake of principle or make as much as he can, regardless of consequences.

Business ethics in our day is rarely a clear-cut black-and-white matter. "Respectable" people hardly ever steal outright, but some may maneuver, wheel and deal, and walk gingerly on the narrow line that separates the illegitimate from the illegal. In an era of big business and corporate structures and interlocking directorates and tax law and labor relations, the opportunities for abuse of the law are greater than ever. The gap between law and ethics continually widens. However much well-intentioned legislatures attempt to contain this gap by revising laws to accord with new conditions, circumvention of the law—disreputable respectability—remains a serious problem for those who want to be moral and legal.

Even though the Talmud, the great body of Jewish legal and moral literature, dealt with the economy of relatively primitive pre-modern Jewish societies, the fundamental issues were the same. The contest between the devious mentality of the profit-seeker and the moral instinct of the men of the law is written on every page of the Talmud. More than in any other branch of law, the Talmudic Sages showed remarkable adaptability in matters of business. The change from an agrarian culture to one of commerce and finance was taken in stride by the Talmud. New questions always came up—and new solutions were always found on the basis of precedent and deduction.

The method of this encounter with new problems changed following the end of the Talmudic period. Two disputants would come before a rabbi or a rabbinical court to present their problem. If it was found to be too difficult, the question would be forwarded to some great and widely acknowledged authority, who would respond with his ruling in a letter called a *teshuvah* in Hebrew or "responsum" in English. Eventually, the authorities published their responsa.

Responsa literature is therefore really the "case history" of Jewish Law. The late Rabbi Yehudah Leib Maimon, a renowned bibliophile and Israel's first Minister of Religions, estimated that in matters of civil and domestic law alone—excluding such topics as Kashrut and Shabbat—there are on record over a hundred thousand such cases. And this includes only those in print, not the very many still in manuscript.

This literature, especially the sections dealing with business ethics, reveals the manner in which the Rabbis, who had spent all their lives in the yeshiva or academy, were equipped to deal with the most intricate problems that men of affairs could devise. They were deeply pious scholars who trained themselves to anticipate the most devious schemes of the dishonest in the marketplace, so as to enable the rule of right and justice to prevail. They were not at all naïve.

RESPONSA (NO. 78)
R. Asher ben Yehiel

This selection illustrates how one major legal thinker dealt with one such problem. R. Asher ben Yehiel ("the Rosh") was a Ger-

man Jew who settled in medieval Spain, thus combining within himself the two traditions of Ashkenazi and Sephardi Jewry. He was exclusively a Talmudist, more in keeping with his German background than with the philosophic and scientific tradition of the Spanish Jews. But he was a man of broad vision and deep insight, qualities that are evident in his famous Commentaries on the Talmud and in his responsa, from which the following selection has been translated.

Worthy of note are the various efforts at circumventing the law, the wide range of precedent cited, and above all the moral impulse that motivates Jewish Law and its renowned expositors.

You asked about Reuben,* who borrowed money from Simeon without giving him a written note or receipt. Thereafter Reuben gave away all his property to Levi, in order to avoid having to pay his debt to Simeon. For Reuben knows that in the absence of a written contract, the lender cannot collect from property that belonged to the borrower at the time the debt was incurred, but was subsequently sold or given away as a gift.

It seems to me that in this case we follow our estimation of Reuben's obvious motives [this judicial assumption is called an umdena, literally: a measurement]. And on that basis we must conclude that after all Reuben's strenuous efforts he has accomplished nothing at all. His case is similar to that of a critically ill man who assigned all his property to another person. Subsequently, he recovered and sought the return of his estate. We declare the gift void because of our umdena: we appraise his intention as having been that the gift was to take place only in the event of his death, which then seemed imminent, and since he recovered and his intention was not fulfilled, the transfer of the property is invalid.

Another such case is that of a man who left his home for overseas and then heard that his only son had died. Whereupon he assigned all his property to a stranger. Later, his son appeared and claimed his father's estate. The Talmud records the opinion of one

* Reuben, Simeon, and Levi are standard nomenclature to identify the parties in a dispute.

teacher that denies the son his father's estate and holds the transfer of property as legal and valid. However, R. Simeon ben Menassia, whose opinion remains Halakhah, declares the father's gift void because of *umdena:* we consider it obvious that had the father known his son was alive, he would never have given away all his money to a stranger. There are many other such illustrations of the Sages' deciding an issue upon the basis of *umdena.*

Now there is hardly a stronger *umdena* than the case under discussion. Reuben, who gave away all his money, obviously had no intention of supporting himself thereafter by begging from house to house. His intention is so obvious as to be self-evident: he seeks to circumvent the law and avoid payment of his debt to Simeon.

But we cannot permit his dishonest scheme to succeed. His deviousness will not help him. Proof comes from the Talmud, *Bava Metzia* 108a. A man who wishes to sell his land must give his immediate neighbors the right of first refusal. They have priority in purchasing from him the land at the same price he would receive from a stranger. This is a moral consideration, for a stranger could buy land elsewhere without injury, whereas the neighbor who wishes to acquire more land would suffer inconvenience if his new lot were not adjacent to his present one. This moral point has the force of law, on the basis of the verse, "You shall do what is right and good in the eyes of the Lord" (Deuteronomy 6:18).

Now the Talmud considers the following problem. If a man bought a lot which was surrounded on all sides by other lots belonging to the same seller, the sale is valid only if the land purchased was either far superior or far inferior to the surrounding land; for then we assume that he had no plans to acquire the adjacent property in addition to his present purchase. However, if the lot was essentially of the same quality as the land around it, then we assume (*umdena*) that the buyer was seeking to circumvent the law of the neighbor's priority. He felt that if the seller would place all his lands for sale on the open market, and he would ask to purchase them, the neighbors would object and assert their rights of first refusal by buying the land themselves. His plan, therefore, is to buy into the area by initially purchasing this lot surrounded on all sides by the seller's other lots. The neighbors can register no objection because this first plot is not adjacent to any of their land.

But then he becomes a "neighbor" to the seller's other property, equally with the original neighbors—so that when the seller is ready to dispose of the remainder of his property, he may acquire it without having to receive permission from them. Since we assume this to be an attempt at deception, we frustrate his designs by allowing the original neighbors to assert their right of first refusal upon the sale of the first lot. Such is the decision of the Talmud.

Now if we employ *umdena,* appraising a man's motives as devious, and deny him the legal means to act on them, in the case cited by the Talmud—then most certainly do we do so in the case under discussion here. For the underlying principle in the Talmud's case, that of a neighbor's prior rights, is only a rabbinical decree derived from the verse "You shall do what is right and good," etc. Even though the principle is only one of rabbinical law, the Sages went to great lengths to uphold it against circumvention. Surely, then, in our case, which involves not merely a rabbinical decree but an attempt to rob by deception and to violate a Biblical precept by not paying a creditor, we must use every means to thwart his plans. We must therefore allow Simeon to collect from Levi the money owed by Reuben.

Another precedent is the case of a slave owned by two partners jointly. If one partner frees his half, the Sages force the other partner to do likewise, so as to avoid the anomaly of a man who is half slave and half free—and is therefore forbidden to marry either a bondswoman or a freewoman. Now the Talmud in *Gittin* 40a records the case of one partner who emancipated his share in a slave. The other partner, afraid that the Rabbis would force him to do the same and thus cause him to lose his investment, promptly sold his half to his minor son. His plan was obvious: the rabbinical courts could not force the new half-owner, the minor son, to liberate his share of the slave, because a minor is disqualified under the law from engaging in any legal acts such as the emancipation of a slave. Rav Joseph ben Rava consulted Rav Pappa, and the latter replied: pay him back in kind, i.e., declare his gift to his minor son as null and void, and then force him to liberate his share of the slave.

From all this we see that when one attempts to circumvent the law, the Talmudic Sages opposed him and sought to nullify his actions. We must therefore compare all new cases to theirs, and learn from their precedents. For the Sages of the Talmud did not record in advance all possibilities of future circumvention. Clearly, in our case where we are dealing with a major law—the payment of a debt—there is hardly a greater *umdena* revealing the underhandedness of Reuben.

I have seen a similar decision in a responsum by my teacher (Rabbi Meir of Rothenburg) concerning real-estate transactions which specified conditions seeking to undermine the *ketubah* [marriage document] rights of the wife of one of the principals. The law grants a woman, upon her marriage, certain rights, which are recorded in the *ketubah*. These assure her first claim, for specified amounts, on the property of her husband in case of his death or their divorce. Now the buyer wants to purchase the real estate on condition that it not be subject to his wife's *ketubah*, so that, for instance, should he divorce her, she could not collect from this property. In a second such instance, a man bought a parcel of land and arranged for the contract to be written in his brother's name, again so as to deprive his wife of her *ketubah* in the case of his death or their divorce. In both cases, our teacher and Rabbi— Meir, of blessed memory—ruled that the wife may indeed sue for her *ketubah* from this property. In appraising their motives (*umdena*) we find that both were obvious attempts to circumvent the rabbinical decree of *ketubah* and we therefore disqualify the conditions attached to the sale.

Peace to you and your study of Torah, in accordance with the wishes of Asher, son of Rabbi Yehiel, may the memory of the righteous be a blessing.

14. Freedom

The Jewish tradition cherishes freedom. A host of important observances commanded in the Torah are legislated *zekher li'yetziat mitzrayim*, "in remembrance of the Exodus from Egypt": observing the Sabbath and the major holidays, loving the stranger, giving to the poor, exercising compassion for the underprivileged, wearing the fringes on certain garments (thus the *tallit*). Freedom was at issue in the Maccabean revolution celebrated at Hanukkah, in the Bar Kokhba revolt, and in the establishment of the State of Israel in our own day.

While this freedom which the tradition seeks to inculcate includes political freedom, it is not confined to it. Thus the Jewish tradition commends the study of Torah as a means of attaining inner spiritual freedom and personal dignity even when the Jew was externally subjugated. Still, the theme of freedom from external restraint, from foreign domination, has been a powerful motif in Jewish history from the Exodus down through to modern times. "For you are servants unto Me," declares the Torah in the name of God, and the Sages add, "but never servants to servants." To accept the yoke of slavery without complaint or resistance is to deny the sovereignty of God to whom, alone, the Jew is obliged to submit.

A contemporary demonstration of the Jewish love of freedom is offered today by the heroic efforts of many Soviet Jews to emigrate to Israel. Despite half a century of Communist indoctrination, enforced ignorance of the Jewish tradition, intense anti-religious propaganda, relentless persecution of Zionism and any expression of Jewish national consciousness, and total deprivation of Jewish spiritual guides, teachers, institutions, and books, impressive numbers of Jews behind the Iron Curtain are demanding their freedom to leave the Soviet Union and make their lives in Israel. The courage with which they have done this, their contempt for personal danger, their recklessness in the face of certain retaliation—these thrusts have given new life to the old-new Jewish belief in freedom.

LETTERS FROM SOVIET JEWS

The literature on Soviet Jewry and their will to be free is rapidly growing. While many eloquent passages could be cited, especially from Elie Wiesel's The Jews of Silence, *the letters from Soviet Jews themselves are becoming major documents in the history of the Jewish people and important expressions of its passion for freedom. They are links in the unbroken chain forged by Moses' challenge to Pharaoh, "Let my people go," the identical words being addressed by Soviet Jews to their government today.*

1. "Let Me Out!"—Boris Kochubiyevsky

On May 16, 1969, a thirty-three-year-old Jewish radio engineer from Kiev was sentenced to three years in a Soviet labor camp for slandering the Soviet system. He had defended Israel at an "anti-Zionist" lecture at his factory, and had drawn attention to the Jewish martyrdom at Babi Yar. This the court found to be "bourgeois-nationalist-Zionist propaganda." He lost his job and his wife was expelled from her university as a "Zionist"; the couple applied for exit visas to Israel. On the day they were to pick up their emigration papers their apartment was raided. On November 28, 1968, Kochubiyevsky wrote the following letter; one week later he was arrested. The trial of Kochubiyevsky took place in the same courthouse in which the trial of Mendel Beilis took place (the protagonist of Bernard Malamud's The Fixer). *The courtroom was packed with anti-Semites, and Kochubiyevsky's brother was jeered outside: "You are a kike, a kike, a kike!"*

I am a Jew. I want to live in a Jewish state. This is my right, as it is the right of a Ukrainian to live in the Ukraine, the right of a Russian to live in Russia, the right of a Georgian to live in Georgia.

I want to live in Israel.

This is my dream, this is the goal, not only of my life but also of the lives of hundreds of generations preceding me that were expelled from the land of their ancestors.

I want my children to study in a school in Yiddish. I want to read Yiddish newspapers. I want to attend a Yiddish theater. What's wrong with that? What is my crime? Most of my relatives were shot by the Fascists. My father perished, and his parents were killed. If they were alive today, they would be standing next to me. *Let me go!*

With this request, I turned repeatedly to various departments and achieved only dismissal from work, my wife's expulsion from her institute, and—to top it all—prosecution, accusing me of slandering the Soviet reality. What is this slander? Is it really a slander that in the multinational Soviet state only the Jewish people cannot educate their children in schools in their own language? Is it really a slander that there isn't a Yiddish theater in the USSR? Is it a slander that there aren't any Yiddish newspapers in the USSR? By the way, nobody denies it. Perhaps it is a slander that for more than a year I haven't been able to leave for Israel? Or a slander that nobody wants to speak to me, that there is nobody to complain to? Nobody reacts. But that is not even the point. I don't want to interfere in the ethnic affairs of a state in which I consider myself an outsider. I want to leave. I want to live in Israel. My wish does not contradict Soviet legislation. I have an invitation from my relatives, all formalities have been observed. Is that why my home was searched?

I am not asking for mercy. Listen to the voice of reason: *Let me out!*

As long as I live, as long as I am capable of feeling, I will do all I can to be able to leave for Israel. And if you find it possible to sentence me for it, then all the same, if I live till my release, I will be prepared to go to the homeland of my ancestors, even if it means going on foot.

2. *Unconquered and immortal* *—The Georgia Eighteen*

On August 6, 1969, the heads of eighteen Jewish families from three cities of the Georgian sector of the USSR jointly sent to the United Nations an appeal of which the following is an excerpt.

We, eighteen religious Jewish families of Georgia, request you to help us leave for Israel. Each of us, upon receiving an invitation from a relative in Israel, obtained the necessary questionnaires from the authorized USSR agencies and filled them out. Each was assured orally that no obstacles would be put in the way of his departure. Expecting to receive permission any day, each sold his property and gave up his job. But long months have gone by—years, for many—and permission for departure has not yet been given. We have sent hundreds of letters and telegrams; they have vanished like tears in the sand of the desert. All we hear are one-syllable oral refusals. We see no written replies. No one explains anything. No one cares about our fate.

For a long time, the Roman legions besieged Jerusalem. But despite the well-known horrors of the siege—hunger, lack of water, disease—the Jews did not renounce their faith and did not surrender. However, man's strength has its limits too, and in the end barbarians broke into the Holy City. Thus, two thousand years ago, the Holy Temple was destroyed—and with it the Jewish State. The nation, however, remained. Although the Jews who could bear arms did not surrender to the enemy and killed one another, there remained the wounded, who were bleeding to death; there remained the old people, women, and children.

And whoever could not get away was killed on the spot.

But whoever could went away into the desert; and whoever survived reached other countries, to believe and pray and wait.

And the Jews had to endure everything. . . . But millions upon millions preferred a life of suffering and often death to apostasy. And even if their ashes are scattered through the world, the memory of them is alive. Their blood is in our veins, and our tears are their tears.

The prophecy has come true: Israel has risen from the ashes; we have not forgotten Jerusalem, and it needs our hands.

There are eighteen of us who signed this letter. But he errs who thinks there are only eighteen of us. There could have been many more signatures.

They say there is a total of twelve million Jews in the world. But he errs who believes there are only twelve million of us. For with those who pray for Israel are hundreds of millions who did not live to this day, who were tortured to death, who are no longer here. They march shoulder to shoulder with us, unconquered and immortal, those who handed down to us the traditions of struggle and faith.

That is why we want to go to Israel.

History has entrusted the United Nations with a great mission —to think about people and help them. Therefore, we demand that the United Nations Human Rights Commission do everything it can to obtain from the Soviet government in the shortest possible time permission for us to leave. It is incomprehensible that in the twentieth century people can be prohibited from living where they wish to live. It is strange that it is possible to forget the widely publicized appeals about the right of nations to self-determination—and, of course, the right of people who comprise the nation.

We will wait months and years, we will wait all our lives if necessary, but we will not renounce our faith or our hopes.

We believe: Our prayers have reached God.

We know: Our appeals will reach humanity.

For we are asking little: Let us go to the land of our forefathers.

3. *To Live for My People—Tina Brodetskaya*

Tina Brodetskaya, a resident of Moscow, addressed the following "open letter" to Premier Aleksei Kosygin in October 1969. Later that month the letter was smuggled out to the West.

I apply to you in an open letter because, to my repeated applications to the Soviet authorities to permit me to emigrate to my relatives in Israel, I have been receiving refusals which, in accordance with the accepted order, are given orally, by telephone, without any statements concerning the reasons for the refusal or concerning the identity of the persons who had made these decisions.

My desire to go to Israel is caused by national feelings alone and not by hostility toward the Soviet Union.

During the Second World War my father, who had volunteered for the front, was killed. Many of my close relatives were also killed. In my early childhood, together with my mother—an army physician—I followed the Soviet troops from the Ukraine to Berlin. I saw German concentration camps, embalmed heads of Jewish officials and crates with soap inscribed: "From Jewish fat." I had to realize why such things happened precisely to the Jews. Later I understood that the defenselessness of the Jews was caused by the absence of a Jewish State and that the fate of Jews really mattered only to the Jewish State.

I decided that there was only one road for me—*to live for my people*. In my student years I endeavored to awaken national feelings in Jews. In 1957 I was sentenced to prison for Zionism. My stay in prison did not change my convictions. I still consider Israel as my national homeland.

I consider that under conditions that make it impossible to express one's national essence and to educate the growing generation in a national spirit, the Jewish people in the USSR is totally doomed to forcible assimilation. *I don't want to assimilate*. My desire to live in Israel is unshakeable. I therefore insistently demand the satisfaction of my natural right to decide my fate for myself and to be allowed to go to Israel.

I have already applied by letters to the leaders of the Soviet government, but in answer I received a postcard with the request to telephone. My phone calls were answered by anonymous persons saying that the right of departure had been refused to me. I am forced to apply to you, Aleksei Nikolayevich, in an open letter, as there is no other way out for me.

4. *Only One Cure*—Joseph Kerler

Fifty-two-year-old Joseph Kerler is a Jewish poet who had been refused exit from the USSR. After having served and been wounded in the Red Army during World War II, he was arrested in 1948 and released in 1954. His poetry, first published in 1944, was reissued in 1959, but he has not been able to publish since 1965. His appeal, which follows, dated November 18, 1969, was sent to Nechama Lifshitz, the Russian Jewish folksinger who managed to leave the USSR in early 1969. The lyrics to many of Miss Lifshitz's songs are by Kerler.

Dearest Nechamele,

As you see, four years have gone by since the authorities granted us an exit permit to join our family in Israel. Unfortunately, however, when all was ready for our departure, the permit was suddenly, and without explanation, nullified. You know very well how these developments have affected our situation and our health. Especially my Anya's health. In the past few years she has twice been hospitalized with dangerous infections and serious heart attacks. Small wonder: it was *she* whose father, mother, brothers, and sisters (eleven souls, all told!) were slaughtered by the fascist beasts. It was she, the lone survivor, who over the many years searched and ultimately found her only remaining relatives in Israel. It was she, a heroic, dedicated nurse, who served on all fronts of the battle against the fascist invader—from Kharkov to Bucharest to Belgrade. And so of course it was she who was hardest hit by the vicious injustice perpetrated against us.

You ask, dear Nechama, what medicines to send for Anya. For Anya, as for all of us, there is one and only one cure—to be reunited with our family in Israel!

Yes, for all of us, this is the right medicine, more indispensable to us than bread, than air.

Dear Nechamele! I am the last person here who wrote Jewish poems for you, and you were the last to sing my songs. Who could grasp my situation as well as you?

I am a Jewish poet and as such I am utterly superfluous in the Soviet Union. Surely no one can any longer deny that because of certain historical developments, there is absolutely no future for Jewish culture here. Without Jewish educational and cultural institutions, without a press, a theater, and, above all, without a mass Jewish readership—what is there for a Jewish writer to do here? It is only natural that a Jewish poet should want to live where his people, his culture, his language are firmly established; where he can be certain that his child will grow up, not as a person of ambiguous nationality but rather as a free, proud, progressive Jew.

Our passionate yearning to go to Israel is natural, lawful, just, and very human!

Does this mean that we are disloyal to the Soviet Union? Absolutely not! Like my wife, I fought actively in the Great Fatherland War, and was wounded several times in battle against the German fascists. This earth, soaked in blood and sweat, is dear to me, is my own. The great culture of Russia is dear to me, is my own. I was reared in its revolutionary, freedom-loving spirit. I love Russian poetry and the Russian landscape. We will never forget the extraordinary sacrifices by which the Soviet people saved humanity in general and the Jewish people in particular from the Brown Plague and extermination.

And yet—we must leave Russia. Better to remain friends from afar. My most ardent desire is to be able to say with a clear heart and a free mind:

> Dear land where I was cradled,
> Farewell,
> I leave you now,
> Not like a beaten dog

Who, at a whistle or a pat
Is pathetically ready to bound back
And wag his tail. . . .
I go with heavy heart,
With leaden steps.
With each step
I tear away
Pieces of earth
Soaked with my blood
I wrench my eye away
I wrench my heart away
And wish you:
Let all be well with you!

After our 1965 permit was revoked we appealed to the highest authorities, but apparently our plea didn't reach that high. . . . This year we applied twice for an exit permit, but after seven months of "being considered," we were twice denied. And once again—without explanations. It goes without saying that we will persevere in our stubborn struggle for our lawful rights. And we feel sure that the Soviet authorities, basing themselves on the highest principles of justice and humanity, will in the end renew our permit.

The question is only—how long will it drag on? The years fly swiftly by and our health is deteriorating. I have not published a single line in four years. You know how hard and bitter it is for us. . . . But we are not asking for pity. All we ask, dearest Nechama, is that you help us knock on all the doors. Perhaps through you our pain, our cry of woe, will reach the highest Soviet authorities.

Remember—we are on the verge of destruction. Yes, destruction—for we have no other way out if the great injustice done our family is not redressed, if our right to emigrate to Israel is not soon restored.

Keep well, Nechamele, our solace and our great hope! I wish you success in all your singing and in all your undertakings. Anya, Berele, and I embrace you, hug you, and kiss you with all our heart.

5. Tell the Story—Michael Zand

After Michael Zand's father, a loyal Communist, was secretly exe-
cuted by the Stalinist regime on a charge of spying for Poland, the
son's disillusionment matured into a hatred of Communist tyr-
anny, a return to Judaism, and a fervent commitment to Zionism
and Israel. Overcoming all difficulties with almost superhuman
courage, Dr. Zand became an internationally distinguished scholar
of Oriental cultures and languages, especially Persian. Even after
his father was "rehabilitated," Dr. Zand made no secret of his
contempt for the Russian government and police. He was a leader
of the "democratic underground" and wrote clandestine Zionist
tracts in Russia. Worldwide pressure from the scholarly commu-
nity finally persuaded the Soviets that it was in their best interests
to let Zand, with his wife and children and mother, emigrate to Is-
rael in May 1971, where Professor Zand now teaches at Bar-Ilan
University. His memoirs, from which the following translation is a
brief excerpt, appeared in the Israeli newspaper Maariv.

My most overwhelming experience during those years was the
Youth Festival in Moscow, in August 1957. When the Israelis
came, when I saw for the first time in my life our strong and
proud young people, our sisters and brothers from the Holy Land,
and the gigantic flag of blue and white (in fact, I had such a flag in
my home—but it was very small, for I had sewn it myself)—I remembered what my grandfather once told me. He was a pious Jew
for whom sports were altogether strange and foreign. Yet when
the Israeli basketball team visited Moscow—I think it was in
1955—he didn't miss a single game. He was highly emotional,
and murmured to me, "I didn't understand a thing. I don't even
know what a 'basket' is. But I looked at our boys, at how strong
they were, and my heart pounded away the words: *'Am yisrael*
hai, The people of Israel lives! *Am yisrael hai!'* " And then
Grandfather said to me, "If ever another group of young Israelis

comes here—go and see them. It's not important what they're doing. Just go and see that *am yisrael hai."*

So I went to see how *am yisrael hai,* and I relived with him those great days. I stood there, on that street in Moscow through which the various delegations had to pass in their trucks. As each group came by, they would call out greetings in their native tongue, and the crowds of Soviet citizens lining the streets would shout back their welcome. So, when the Arab delegation called out *"Salaam, salaam,"* the crowds thundered in response, *"Salaam, salaam."* From the distance I noticed our two trucks. The first was reserved only for Communist members of the Israeli delegation, the second for the others. My heart was on fire. When the trucks approached us, we heard the cries of *"Shalom, shalom, shalom."* And the street—the street was silent, struck dumb! Not a single sound. I took a deep breath and filled my lungs with air. I stretched out my throat and shouted with all my strength, almost till I lost my senses, *"Shalom, shalom, shalom to Israel."* People standing around me looked at me as if I were crazy and began moving away from me, lest anyone suspect them, Heaven forbid, of having uttered those terrible words. But around me I heard silent whispers: *"Shalom, shalom"*—while those who recited them lowered their eyes and turned about so as not to attract any attention. . . .

When I was appointed head of the Literature and Culture Department of a bimonthly journal for Oriental studies, they began to pressure me to join the Communist Party. The people at the Party office argued that only one who is ideologically perfect could be trusted in such a sensitive position. I argued, in turn, that I did not want to become a member of the Party and that I had no interest in political matters. I saw that I could talk openly to the secretary of the Party cell in the editorial staff of the journal, so I said to him, "This is not my country and this is not my Party, so let me alone!" He didn't inform on me, but the pressure kept up incessantly. At the same time, I did not derive any real satisfaction from my work, which was primarily editing, while I longed for research. After much effort, I was permitted to leave the bimonthly and I was transferred to the Oriental Institute. Here I got a lowly position at half the salary of my previous job. But there was no let-up in the pressure on me to join the Party. All my arguments that one doesn't have to be a Party member to undertake research in medieval literature were to no avail. Finally, I became disgusted with all this pressure and exploded with the words, "Go to the devil! I will never join and I don't care what you do to me!" Only then did they let me alone. . . .

I wanted very much to establish contact with foreign scholars, especially Jews, in order to let the world know, through them, what was happening to Soviet Jewry. That is why I was so disappointed when the regime turned down five invitations from Iran for me to come to Iran to lecture at universities on Persian studies. But salvation came in 1966. There took place in Teheran the first international conference on Iranian studies. The Soviet Union put together a large delegation of twelve scholars, and fortunately I was included. Under these conditions the authorities were less apprehensive about me, because the "scientific" delegation included members of the KGB [secret police], who would keep a careful eye on me and listen in on all my conversations. My family, of course, remained behind in Moscow, and the authorities knew that I would do nothing which might hurt them. But despite all their precautions, I succeeded in making important contact in Persia with two distinguished scholars, both Jews, one from the United States and one from England.

I had heard much while I was in Moscow about the American, Professor Herbert Feifer, and I had read his works. I did not know that he was a Jew. Our first conversation took place one morning in a bus that was taking us from the Teheran Hilton to Teheran University. We became acquainted and exchanged impressions in English. It turned out that he knew me from my writings. At the noontime break that day, we left the hall together and when we were some distance from it, he turned to me and said, "Do you by any chance speak Yiddish too?"

I was startled. "And you?"

"What then? I swear I'm Jewish!"

From that moment on we adopted Yiddish as our language and we very much enjoyed each other's company. I spoke with him extensively on many Jewish subjects. I told him about the hapless Jews in the Soviet Union, about the anti-Semitism and the great dream of tens and hundreds of thousands of Jews to emigrate to Israel.

In one of my conversations with Professor Feifer I told him that I learned Hebrew from various books I had found here and there, and that it was a pity he did not speak the language, for I could have used the opportunity to brush up on my spoken Hebrew. Feifer said to me, "One minute. There's another one of our people here, Professor Bernard Lewis of England, and he knows Hebrew and would be glad to talk with you in that language."

That was indeed a complete joy to me. The crowning event of this "Jewish underground" in Teheran took place when all the delegations were invited to meet the Shah in his palace. We shook hands, according to protocol, exchanged a few polite words—and then Feifer and Lewis and I went off into a corner, not too far from the other Soviet delegates, with the Shah sitting right next to us. We spoke Yiddish and Hebrew with open glee. We were especially delighted by the fact that we were "making history": it was the first time in the history of the Persian palace that three Jews were sitting there, conversing in Hebrew and Yiddish!

From my fellow scholars I requested only one thing: *Tell the story!* Tell it in your countries and tell it in Israel when you get there, tell them about the agony of Soviet Jewry and demand of the Free World that it not remain silent, that it raise its voice in protest.

Professor Lewis told me that he expected to go to Jerusalem for a series of lectures, and I said to him, in Hebrew, "To be in Jerusalem—that is the greatest dream of my life. Greet Jerusalem in my name, kiss its soil for me. And tell the people at the University in Jerusalem that there is a man in Moscow who would be the happiest man in the world if he could go to Jerusalem for only a single day; and if that were impossible—then he would settle for twelve hours." . . .

On the 24th of March (1971), after I officially requested permission to go on *aliyah* to Israel, I participated in a sitdown strike at the home of the President of the Supreme Soviet. I was one of five Jews, representatives of Moscow Jewry, who talked with the head of the reception department. The next day, I returned to demonstrate in the same place.

The day after that I was expelled from the Soviet Academy of Sciences. That did not prevent me from joining a strike, that afternoon, at the office of the public prosecutor of Moscow. Forty of us participated. We demanded an answer to our protest against their intentions to try Jews in criminal cases [for wanting to go to Israel].

At night they arrested us. They took us to the jail where they keep drunks, taken off the streets. Eight of us, including me, were held over till the morning, when the police conducted lightning trials. Mine lasted fifteen seconds. "You are a hooligan," I was told, and sentenced to fifteen days in jail. After three days in the police jail, where we slept on the floor and the cold cut through our bones, they took us to the famous prison in Moscow for criminal convicts.

Immediately after the verdict at the "trial," we declared a full hunger strike. I drank only water, and continued the strike even in prison. They took me in for a medical examination—and there I met a man whom, though he would not tell me his name, I thought of as "Dr. Mengele," after the notorious Nazi murderer of the concentration camps. Every movement, every word, reminded me of him. He had an intellectual look, and was dressed in white. He was honest, and made no bones of the fact that my life meant nothing to him. "We are going to feed you by force," he said. "I don't care if you die or not, but you will eat." I thought to myself: *You shall not win over me, because despite my hunger, despite my weak physical condition, despite the fact that I am a member of a small and oppressed people—I am stronger than you because my cause is just, because I am a Jew!* Thereupon I wrote out a complaint against his threat. I gave two reasons for my refusal: first, my ulcer and liver disease. Second, I said, I am an observant, religious Jew, and I must recite the *birkhat hamazon* [grace] after the meal; but how can I do so if I am fed against my will?

Two days later they took me back to Dr. Mengele. He examined me and shouted, "You are going to eat! Yes, I read your complaint and I'm not scared. We shall force the food down you, and if you die in the process we shall record that due to an unfortunate accident you were taken off the list of the living—with no more ceremony than defective products are removed from a factory." I answered, "I thought that every doctor was first of all a human being who does not relate to people as to spoiled products that are superfluous. Now, only now, I know that a doctor in a Soviet jail is not at all a human being." He looked at me with cold eyes and said, "Now you know it. You are going to learn many more new things."

On the twelfth day of the hunger strike, when I was quite weak, two policemen came and told me that the prosecutor had invited me to discuss my complaint against the doctor's threats. I had by then decided upon total resistance, with whatever strength I had left in me, to any forced feeding. I didn't believe the policemen; still, I went with them. They took me to a room, where I was confronted by an array of people: Mengele, and next to him a woman in army uniform and white shirt, apparently a nurse, five powerfully built policemen, and another doctor. Next to them were all kinds of instruments, tubes, and a large glass bottle of food. Mengele spoke: "We are prepared to feed you by force. For the last time, we suggest you eat voluntarily."

"No," I answered.

"If we feed you by force," Mengele asked, "will you resist us?"

"With all my strength," I answered.

"Take him out," screamed Mengele.

A few minutes later they brought me back in. Two of the policemen held my hands and the third tried to push me down onto the bed. I was weak, but I tried to resist, to wrestle with them. They began to twist my arms. I had advanced standing in Judo, so I started to laugh because one of them had an entirely wrong grip on me. This offended me. I told him that he was doing his job in a very unprofessional manner. Two other cops sat on my feet and another man sat on my thigh. He was gray-haired and older than the rest. He looked like a hangman and had considerable experience in torture from the days of Stalin. They covered my face tightly with a towel so that I could not move it.

Mengele stood above me, cold as ice. "For the last time, yes or no?" I shook my head to indicate my negative answer. First they gave me intravenous injections. Then they brought over the big glass bottle, to the bottom of which was connected a large rough rubber tube. The nurse started to push the tube into my nose. "It won't go in," she said to Mengele, "it's too thick." Mengele was brief: "In it goes!" She pushed with all her might, but its diameter was three times that of my nostril. I heard the bones of my nose breaking. Mengele smiled. The doctor was satisfied. They put some white, milky substance into the bottle. The nurse asked, "Doctor, in small doses or all at once?"

"All at once," Mengele answered.

It began to pour into me and I felt I was choking. I gasped for air, and was sure I would die on that bed—which was just what Mengele wanted. I opened my mouth and spat out the thick doughy stuff right into the face of the "hangman." "Shut his mouth," Mengele ordered. It was terrible torture.

"Now will you eat?" asked Mengele. Half dead, I answered with my remaining strength, "No!"

"Then tomorrow we'll feed you again. We're going to break you!" I said: "No! You can break my nose and you can break my hands, *but you can't break my spirit.* I am the son of a stiff-necked people. Read our Bible and you will know."

But they didn't try it again. Three days later I was freed. I was sick and spent. Only the faith that I would somehow reach my Israel kept me going. . . .

On April 28, 1971, I was called to a meeting at the Ovir offices. Two generals were sitting there, and they called my daughter a traitor and me a hooligan. There was a police officer, of the rank of general, and he screamed at me, "Hooligan! You will never receive permission to go to Israel!" I recognized him from a previous meeting, when we conducted a strike at the Ministry of the Interior. I said to him, "We shall go up on *aliyah!* I am absolutely certain of that. You can play around with us, delay us, postpone it again and again, laugh at us and ridicule us—but we shall go up!"

When the general argued that I couldn't back up my claim that I wanted to emigrate in order to reunite the family, and that I had no relatives in Israel, I said to him, "Since you are all here experts on the Jewish question, you might as well know that with us

Jews the concept of 'family' is much broader than it is with you. All the Jews of Israel are my close relatives!"

On May 10, 1971, my heart jumped for joy. They gave me permission to go to Israel.

Four days later they rescinded the permit. They called me back to Ovir and took away my papers. I ran, wrote, protested. I asked the government of Israel for Israeli citizenship. I wrote to the Secretary General of the UN and signed, "A Former Citizen of the USSR." I bombarded every government office of the Soviet Union with my protests. I was burning to leave, I could stand it no longer.

Finally, they let me go. And here I am. In Jerusalem. If I tell you that I'm happy, that I'm floating on clouds, that sometimes I wake up in the morning afraid to open my eyes because I'll discover the whole thing is only a dream and really I'm back there, in Moscow—I will not have begun to tell you anything. Because there are no words. There are no words.

15. Leadership

The relationship between established leadership and the community, including the disadvantaged and underprivileged, is the subject of political and social theories. In our own times, it has become the focus of powerful protest and restlessness. From the Old Left to the New Left, from Marx to Marcuse, this problem has aroused passions and sparked new movements.

It would be naïve to expect Judaism to have a clear-cut opinion on all such political and social situations of our day. But we do have the views of Tzvi Hirsch Kaidanower, a deeply religious personality, whose reactions to the challenges of his own society in Eastern Europe over two and a half centuries ago are still of interest.

The realities and the power structure of that time and place were far different from conditions in the contemporary world. But certain underlying human attitudes and social configurations remain fundamentally unchanged. Then as now, power bred arrogance, the poor were hungry and humiliated, the community had not found an adequate way to care for its disadvantaged.

THE JUST MEASURE
Tzvi Hirsch Kaidanower

Tzvi Hirsch Kaidanower was not a revolutionary. He had and wanted no power base from which to challenge the status quo. Yet he fearlessly upbraided the Jewish community leaders for their failures and called upon them to change their ways. His only authority was the moral and spiritual rectitude of his charges and his demands.

He published his Kav Ha-Yashar (The Just Measure) *in 1705 and it is typical of the Jewish devotional and ethical literature known as Musar.**

Kaidanower's book treats the very real social problems in the Polish Jewish community of the seventeenth century. The mood is somber, rigorous, mystical—but so was Jewish life gloomy, difficult, and pious. Despite this atmosphere, the continuing Jewish concern for justice and compassion comes through.

The author's references to taxation require a word of explanation. During the Middle Ages and much later, the secular government would levy a collective tax upon the Jewish community. It expected the Jewish kahal, *the community organization, to decide upon its own method of taxation and asked only that it deliver the proper sum. Furthermore, the Jewish communal authorities used this power of taxation in order to provide for the special services required within the Jewish community. This semi-autonomy permitted Jews to lead their own lives and order their own affairs as long as they discharged their collective obligation to the secular government. Yet it also opened the door to abuses by those in power, from whom there often was no appeal for relief or remedy.*

The author paints a rather black picture of the economic and social exploitation of the Jewish masses by the communal authorities. There is undoubted overstatement in the indictment; hyperbole is, after all, an accepted part of the technique of ethical preaching, going all the way back to the Prophets. But his sense of

* See Chapter 2, pp. 24 ff.

outrage, his indignant protest, his fearless rebuke of the powers of his society make this an important expression of Jewish social ethics.

I shall now offer a reason for the term *nesiim,* which the Bible uses to describe the leaders and heads of the people.

If a man is worthy and conducts himself in a God-fearing manner, he is elevated or raised high. *Naso* means to elevate, and *nesiim,* therefore, means "those who are elevated." Furthermore, in the world-to-come his soul gains immortality on the same level as the holy and the righteous.

However, if a man does not conduct himself properly, he will vanish without a trace, as do the *nesiim,* the clouds and the wind. This term too is from the Hebrew verb *naso,* which means "to carry." The clouds are carried from one place to another. Just as the clouds evaporate and as the wind disappears, never to return, so too will the community leader whose behavior is unbecoming that of a leader of Israel. One who does not willingly share in the burdens of his people, one who is arrogant toward them, will quickly depart from this world and no trace will be left of his descendants.

Many leaders are ensnared in this trap because of their vanity and superciliousness. They cast a spell of fear upon the community, but do not do so for the sake of Heaven. They take luxuries and pleasures for themselves but do not share in the various taxes to which all others are subject. Indeed, they make life easier for themselves while increasing the burden of others. They are the first to take all kinds of honor and glory for themselves. Their faces are always ruddy from excess drink, and they are physically strong and healthy, indulging every desire of their hearts. They fail to share in the toil of their fellow men and in the difficulties of others.

Meanwhile, the congregation of the Lord, the descendants of Abraham, Isaac, and Jacob, are oppressed and trampled underfoot. They are forced to go naked and barefoot because of the heavy taxes levied on them. The community officials mercilessly enter the homes of the ordinary citizens, divest them of whatever they find, despoil them of all they have, and see to it that they remain without clothing or possessions. They seize even the *tallit* and *kittel,* the prayer shawl and robe. They then sell these objects cheaply, even people's quilts, so that their victims remain with nothing but the straw of their beds. Then when the weather turns cold and the rains come, all shiver; husband, wife, and children —each stays in his own corner, weeping.

Were the leaders to help and participate in paying the taxes, the burden would not be so great upon the middle class and the poor. Thus, an even greater sin is committed by these community leaders who eat and drink at the expense of the community, who give ample dowries to their sons and daughters and gifts to bride and groom, all from public funds. This is money stolen from the hard-won earnings of their fellow Jews.

Concerning a leader or official of this kind, a divine voice issues forth, declaring, "This is the man who devours the flesh and blood of the people of Israel; he steals from the poor, the orphans, the widows." Furthermore, the voice curses him with many maledictions, so that his prayer is never accepted (May the Lord spare us such punishment!).

Therefore, let the man who is a leader or official of the community take care to be compassionate, and never cruel, especially toward those who are as "broken vessels," that is, the poor and the needy. Let him remember that God protects the honor of the destitute, and that if one, Heaven forbid, oppresses them, this arouses evil decrees.

We read of this in the writings of the Ari, R. Isaac Luria, of blessed memory: Once the Ari was sitting together with his disciples in a field in which the Prophet Hosea was buried. He was expounding the mysteries of the Torah, but in the middle of his exposition he turned to his disciples and said: "For God's sake, let us hurry and collect money for *tzedakah* [charity] and send it to a certain poor man who lives nearby. He, R. Jacob Altruz, is sitting and weeping, crying out to God in bitter complaint about his terrible poverty. His voice reaches the utmost heights, splitting all the heavens, and reaches the innermost Presence of God. The Holy

One, blessed be He, is filled with wrath against the whole city of Safed on his account, for we have neglected to deal with him compassionately.

"I hear a divine voice proclaiming throughout all the heavens the decree of God that a heavy plague of locusts shall come upon all of Safed and its environs. It will destroy all the fruit of the field, the vineyards, and the olive trees. Make haste, therefore, and let us send the *tzedakah* to him. Perhaps we can yet succeed, with the help of God, in abrogating the evil decree."

Immediately thereupon, each of the disciples gave his contribution. The Ari then gave the sum to his student, R. Isaac Ha-Kohen, commanding him to hurry at once to the home of R. Jacob Altruz and give him the money. Isaac Ha-Kohen did so immediately and speedily, hurrying to the home of R. Jacob Altruz. He found the poor man at the entrance of his house, weeping and praying to God.

Said R. Isaac, "Rabbi, why do you weep?"

R. Jacob explained that his water jug had broken, and that he did not have a penny with which to buy another one to replace it. His poverty was so terrible, so overwhelming, that he simply did not know what to do. R. Isaac Ha-Kohen immediately gave him the money that was collected for him. R. Jacob was exceedingly happy and blessed all of them because of it.

When R. Isaac returned to his master, the Ari, the latter said that the decree of the locusts had been abrogated and that there was no longer any cause for concern. While they were in the midst of this conversation, a very great wind began to blow and it carried the locusts very, very far away. The disciples were greatly frightened, but the Ari said to them: Do not be afraid, for the evil decree has been revoked. And so it was. All the locusts were carried away by the wind to the Mediterranean Sea, where they drowned. Not a single one remained in the entire area of Safed.

That is the story related in the writings of the Ari.

From this we derive a powerful lesson for all Jews. We must pay very special attention to the poor and the indigent, for they are referred to as "broken vessels," i.e., they are broken-hearted, and the Holy One, blessed be He, dwells amongst them. Indeed, our Rabbis, of blessed memory, taught us that if one gives money or food to a poor man, he is blessed six times, but if he encourages him by speaking to him warmly and tenderly, he is blessed eleven times. It is the heart of the poor man which sighs constantly, for it cannot fully attain that which his body needs. It yearns for the good things which it does not have.

When the cold of winter arrives, the rich man sits like a prince, while the stove warms his special well-built house. Meanwhile, the poor man suffers not only a dwelling place full of cracks and holes, but he cannot even afford to buy wood to warm his body sufficiently. The cold breaks his body and his soul and those of the members of his household. When it rains, the water pours into his house and drips down his neck. All the days of a poor man are spent in misery, by day and by night. He and his family sigh and groan. Nevertheless, they faithfully accept all this with love.

And when the Sabbath and festivals arrive—the time when one should enjoy himself with good food and drink and clean clothing —the poor man remains without bread; and with all this, he offers praise and thanksgiving to God.

The rich man marries off his sons and daughters to whomever he wishes. The poor man, powerless, is forced to marry off his children to anyone available, even if he be a boor without a trace of Torah or piety. It is as if he had bound his daughter and cast her before a lion. His own eyes see how this boor strikes her every day, how she suffers untold anguish. Who can describe the bitterness and the misery of the poor man! Yet the poor man who accepts the lot of his poverty with love shall not be subject to the fires of Hell, and his reward shall be very great. For the poor man is considered as if he were dead in this world and he therefore shall be spared punishment in the next world.

Therefore I warn everyone who gives money to a poor man in the time of his distress not to embarrass him, Heaven forbid, for it is bad enough that he must suffer from his poverty. Rather, as I have said above, one ought to give *tzedakah* when no one is watching. If he gives him the money directly, he should do so in a manner that will pacify the recipient and afford him the opportunity of pouring out his heart in speech.

When one offers hospitality to a visitor, he should likewise do so with a happy mien. It is well known that our Rabbis declared proper hospitality to men worthier even than a reception of the Divine Presence.

Let us return to our subject: a great admonition directed to the leader of the community that he not intimidate the public excessively; that he pay his taxes like any other member of the community or citizens of the state; that he not use flattery to obtain special privileges for his property or family, thereby making heavier the yoke that is laid upon the poor and the needy.

Let the leader act in this manner, and then the Lord will do his will, prosper him, give him children and long life. Amen.

A man should take heed that when he makes a banquet at the occasion of the performance of a *mitzvah*—such as a circumcision or betrothal or wedding or Bar-Mitzvah—that he include among his invited guests the poor and the destitute, and that he take care to speak pleasantly to them. For if one makes such a party for his son or daughter and fails to invite the poor, then the wicked Lilith and Samael raise accusations against him and they bring pain and other evil times upon him.

That is what the Midrash teaches us concerning the banquet prepared by our father Abraham. The story of the *Akedah* [the binding of Isaac by Abraham as a sacrifice] is introduced with the words, "after these *devarim*" (Genesis 22:1). Usually *devarim* means "things"; but it can also mean "words." Here, the Midrash says, it refers to the words of accusation spoken by Satan against Abraham about the "great feast" he had made at the time Isaac was weaned (Genesis 21:8). To this feast Abraham had invited all the great men of his generation—but no poor men were included. Satan's charges against Abraham were accepted, and the Holy One said to Abraham, "Take your son, your only son, your beloved, even Isaac . . . and offer him up as a burnt offering" (*ibid.,* 22:2). It was as a result of this episode that Sarah died, as the Torah goes on to relate.

We find the same thing concerning Job. He made a banquet for his sons, but neglected to invite poor people. As a result Satan kept accusing Job before God, until he caused the death of Job's sons and daughters and took away from him his wealth and his cattle. He did not rest until he brought upon him great personal suffering.

Therefore, let everyone who makes a feast remember to invite the poor, so that the accuser [Satan] may no longer accuse. To the contrary, as we are told in Midrash Tanhuma, when a man does invite the poor to participate in his feast, then his accusers become his defenders.

16. Self-Government

Between the years 70 C.E. and 1948, Jews had no independent state. Whatever talents for statecraft they possessed were expended on behalf of the nations in which they resided. It would seem reasonable to assume that Jewish law, philosophy, and tradition concerning Jewish self-government were arrested during the first century of the Common Era.

Yet, that is not the case. Until the advent of the modern era, most Jewish communities were not integrated into their host countries, although a relationship did exist between the secular government and the Jewish community as such, through which all financial and civic obligations of individual Jews were filtered, and which therefore retained a large measure of autonomy in the conduct of its internal affairs. This was true of most Jewish communities of Christian Europe and the Arab world during the Middle Ages. Since most were usually headed by rabbis or scholars, a study of the way such groups governed themselves reveals the manner in which Judaism and the Jewish tradition exerted a political influence on Jewish society.

Gradually, many of these small autonomous communities endeavored to unite in larger countrywide organizations. What is noteworthy is the way in which persecuted people, dominated by petty local barons often bent on extricating from them as much revenue as possible, managed not only to retain a healthy inner structure but also to cross boundary lines in order to strengthen their semi-governmental machinery and broaden their jurisdiction.

New communal problems were faced and solved through periodic conferences, or synods, which devised methods to enforce old decrees, legislate new ones, and make determinations of how these precarious communities should relate to the secular governments and Gentile populations. Communal rules and decrees (*takkanot*) were often recorded in the communities' registries, or *pinkasim,* which are documents rich in information on Jewish history. The synods usually had no legal standing in the eyes of the host governments; their authority had to be granted voluntarily by the Jews in the respective communities. Only in Spain and Italy were there any official relations between state and synod.

The outstanding personality in the history of Jewish self-government in the Middle Ages was R. Gershom ben Judah of Mayence (960–1040), known as Rabbenu Gershom, "The Light of the Exile." Before the tenth century Jews in the Rhine country had organized themselves into democratic communities, largely self-governing, and had developed a number of new institutions in response to the changing economic, social, and political conditions of their times. Rabbenu Gershom welded together at least three of these smaller communities into one large confederation governed largely by a constitution formulated by his colleagues and himself, all of them rabbis who combined Torah scholarship with the practical vision of accomplished statesmen.

Their influence continued into the eleventh century, when the leading figure became the renowned Rashi (Rabbi Simon ben Isaac), a great commentator on Bible and Talmud. In the next century leadership was exerted by Rashi's grandson, R. Jacob Tam (Rabbenu Tam). By the thirteenth century the position of German Jewry had begun to deteriorate. While it is hard to pinpoint cause and effect, it seems clear that the persecutions to which German Jewry was subject sapped its vitality, reduced its numbers, and generally impoverished it. Synods became much less frequent, and creativity less evident.

By the beginning of the seventeenth century, however, a renaissance of Jewish communal self-government took place. The *tak-*

kanot of a council convened in Frankfort in 1603, the original Hebrew transcript of which was found and published by Markus Horowitz of that city in 1897, are reminiscent of the authority of the earlier German rabbis, in their boldness, fearlessness, and willingness to use all the authority the Jewish law permits the sages of each generation in order to administer the inner affairs of their communal life.

Those *takkanot,* of which this selection is an abstract, speak of equitable and honest taxation, of discouraging Jews from taking their litigations to the secular courts; of prohibiting counterfeiting, usury, and deceit of Gentiles; of reinforcing various parts of the *kashrut* law, such as insuring the proper qualifications of the *shohet* (ritual slaughterer), forbidding Jews from using wine prepared by a Gentile. Their publication brought down upon the Jews the accusation of high treason, a charge which reveals a great deal about medieval German anti-Semitism. In order to refute the charges, three German translations were prepared and circulated. Although the accusations were ultimately dropped, German Jewry, especially Frankfort Jewry, went through a trying, anxious period that lasted several years.

The Council of 1603 was a heroic effort which, unfortunately, did not last. The general deterioration initiated by the Black Plague and the persecutions from the middle of the fourteenth century on had taken their toll.

DECREES OF THE SYNOD OF FRANKFORT

These takkanot *of Frankfort in 1603 represent a cross-section of the concerns, attitudes, and problems dealt with by learned expositors of Jewish law grappling with the realities of social political, religious, and economic life.*

The heads of the communities have gathered here at Frankfort at the order of our masters, the Sages of Germany, to sit in council and look into the needs of the community and to make such ordinances and decrees as appear to be needed by the time and the place, so that the Holy People may not be as sheep without a shepherd.

Section 1

Regarding law and judgment: It is a common offense among the people of our generation to refuse to submit to Jewish law; they even force opposing litigants to present themselves before secular courts. The result is that the Holy Name is profaned and that the government and the judges are provoked at us. We have therefore decided that anyone who sues his neighbor in secular courts shall be compelled to free him from all the charges made against him, even though the courts decided in favor of the plaintiff. A person guilty of taking a case to Gentile courts shall be separated from the community of Israel, shall not be called to the Torah, and shall not be permitted to marry until he repents and frees his fellow from the power of the Gentile courts. If the defendant had to undertake expenditures in order to bring the infraction of this ordinance before the Jewish courts, the offender shall pay the expenses.

It is well known that many persons have by the power of their wealth sought to break down the organization of Jewish life in Germany, and have all but destroyed it completely. It is hoped that at some future time they will be brought to justice. However, anyone who will henceforth act in violation of the above ordinance shall be considered an informer and be ostracized as described above. We have ordained and established a special prayer concerning this rule to be publicly recited in every Jewish community every Sabbath throughout Germany.

If the transgressor of this ordinance be a scholar, he is guilty of profanation of the [Divine] Name, and shall therefore lose his right to be called *rabbi;* anyone who gives him the title shall be punished. If he be a leader or head of a community or an acting rabbi or teacher, he shall be removed from office.

Since we know that we have in our communities wicked men of much influence who cannot be dealt with by the local courts, we

have established five central courts in the following cities—
Frankfort, Worms, Fulda, Friedburg, and Ginzburg. If any local
court finds itself powerless to deal with any person it shall refer
the matter to the district court. The judge of this court shall do all
in his power to bring the offending person to terms.

Section 2

It has been agreed that each settlement shall make the assessment
for the purposes of taxation in the following manner. Each community shall choose assessors of unquestioned honesty and piety,
who will assess all men and women according to their possessions.
The assessors shall take an oath to act without consideration of
friendship or enmity, and to be fair to each person. After making
the assessment they shall divide it in half, and each person shall
pay a "shekel" pro rata on the remainder.

Such persons as live far away from Jewish communities shall be
obliged to present themselves before the community with which
they are generally associated and they shall there be assessed in
the manner just described.

The assessors shall keep the assessments of the individuals in
confidence so far as possible.

The rabbis of Germany have agreed to collect each month beginning with the month of Tishri, 5365 [1605], a tax of one per-
cent of all the property.

The following cities were appointed centers to which collected
moneys were to be sent: Frankfort, Worms, Mayence, Bing,
Hamm, Friedburg, Schneitach, Wallerstein, and Ginzburg.

The assembled delegates shall then choose representative men to
present the Jewish affairs before the court of the King.

The collected moneys shall be put in a treasury, a key to which
shall be in the possession of each of the delegates. But no one
shall remove anything without the knowledge and consent of his
colleagues.

If any persons refuse to give their allotted share toward the
common fund, the head of the court and the head of the community shall be obliged to separate them from the whole community

of Israel, refrain from intermarrying with them, and prohibit them from taking part in any religious function.

It was further agreed that from this day forth no community shall be permitted to withhold its apportioned share of the tax, whether in whole or in part, because of any claim which that community may have against the general organization; but the payment of the tax shall be made, and then the claim adjusted by the Sages of the time.

Section 3

It is often found that men are engaged in *Shehitah* [ritual or kosher slaughtering] who lack adequate authorization; or who having received authorization fail to review their studies and so forget the law. Thus they cause their fellow Jews to eat forbidden food. Moreover, many fail to examine the knife in the proper manner. We therefore urge the head of each province and settlement to send an investigator, so far as possible, to review the necessary laws with the *shohatim*.

Section 4

We have further decided that every head of a community has it as his duty to interfere with the buying of wine from Gentiles. If it is proven that any Jew has drunk wine in the house of a Gentile, it shall be forbidden for any other Jew to marry his daughter, or to give him lodging, or to call him to the Torah, or to allow him to perform any religious function.

We have further decided that every Jew living in a wine-growing province shall make his own wine both for his own use and for sale. One shall not be permitted to keep wine of Gentiles in the same room as properly prepared wine.

The head of the courts of the communities shall make laws regarding this matter as stringent as they may consider fit, and we will assist them in the enforcement of these rules. Any rabbi who commits any infraction of this law shall be deposed from his position, and punishment is decreed against anyone who shall there-after call him *rabbi* or *haver* [a Talmudic title used for scholars; in medieval Germany it was a layman's title of honor, given for knowledge of the Talmud and Halakhah].

Section 5

No one shall be appointed a rabbi without the consent of three heads of academies; the authorization as *haver* given any person by a rabbi outside of Germany shall not be considered valid; no authorization as rabbi shall be given any young man who has not been married for at least two years.

Section 6

It is well known that much trouble has arisen in Jewish communities and settlements because of the wicked Jews who engage in trade of counterfeit coins, the coins in some cases being completely valueless, in other cases designed to look like more valuable ones.

As a result, instead of its being said, "The remnant of Israel does no evil," the Gentiles say, "Where is the God of this nation?" We have therefore agreed that from this day forth anyone found engaged in such practices shall be punished with all the severity described above. This shall also apply to those who forge documents in collecting debts.

Section 7

We have agreed that anyone who buys any wares from one who is well known as a thief or lends a thief money on any pledge, shall be punished in the manner described above.

Section 8

Anyone who borrows money or wares from Gentiles with the intention of failing to pay for them shall also be ostracized in the manner described, and no Jew shall buy any wares from him or have any commerce with him.

Moreover, if he is imprisoned for such an act, no Jew will be permitted to defend him, so that the Gentiles may know that we are not generally guilty of such corrupt practices.

Section 9

We beg of every rabbi who is not a member of this council to agree to these decisions and sign his name to them, and if he finds any persons disobedient to these ordinances to refuse to permit such men to marry within the community. Any rabbi who performs a wedding for those who disobey these ordinances, and also those who intermarry with them, shall be punished and will be considered among those who separate themselves from the community.

Section 10

Any Jew who drinks milk bought from a Gentile [prohibited because of the fear that the Gentile might have mixed the cows' milk with the milk of a non-kosher animal], when the milking was not witnessed by a Jew, shall be punished so that no Jew will eat from any of his dishes, and his friends and neighbors shall be obliged to give information concerning him to the nearest rabbi. If the transgressor be a scholar or a teacher or the head of a court or the president of a community, he shall be removed from his position.

Section 11

Whereas we have noticed that many Jews wear clothing made after the manner of the Gentiles, and we have also noticed that many dress themselves and their daughters in costly clothes, therefore have we decreed by fiat that within thirty days after hearing this decree each community shall take action in this matter. They shall also take action against wearing clothes of mixed linen and wool, and also against usury, both prohibited by the law.

Section 12

No Jew in our provinces shall be permitted to publish any book, new or old, at Basel or any other city in Germany, without the permission of three courts; if anyone transgresses this law and publishes the books without permission, no man shall buy the books under the punishment of excommunication.

Section 13

No rabbi or head of a court shall extend his jurisdiction over communities or districts which are traditionally subject to another court; if any men refuse to obey the orders of their [proper] court and prefer to choose their own rabbi for themselves, both they and that rabbi or teacher shall be excommunicated until the heads of the provinces are reconciled to them.

If any court declares punishment against any transgressors by authority of our ordinances, all Jews shall be obliged to obey the order of the court.

We have decreed that any excommunication or other decree from any rabbi outside of Germany against any Jews in Germany shall be invalid.

Whatever sum is decided upon by us as necessary shall be collected each year, and each person shall pay the sum assessed against him. If any Jews fail to give their share and disobey the agent of the general community, their names shall be announced in every community in Germany. The announcement shall take this form: "The following men, who are mentioned by name, have been separated from the remainder of the Dispersion. They may not mingle or intermarry with us, neither they nor their children, and no person may recite for them the benedictions of the wedding ceremony. If anyone transgresses this order and does marry them, whether he act willingly or under compulsion, the marriage is declared void."

If any member of our people goes before a Gentile court, and the leaders of the community find it impossible to compel him to obey Jewish courts, announcement shall immediately be made concerning him in all the communities so as to compel him to present himself before the court of Frankfort or Worms or Friedburg, or to any court which the defendant will select. If one who is found guilty in this manner fails to repent within thirty days of the announcement, he shall be compelled to pay a fine to the charity fund and to the government, the amount to be decided by the judges. If this will not be sufficient to bring him to terms, we shall seek permission from the government to do justice and to compel the guilty one to defray all the expenses.

17. Other Religions

Contemporary society prides itself on its pluralism, and most of us are in regular contact with men of other religions, other races, often of other nationalities, and certainly of opinions far different from our own. With all the worry about conformity in our society we are daily exposed to many more alternate ways of living than was possible a few generations ago. Yet what is often at stake in these encounters is an individual's right to be and remain different from others. While "pluralism" would seem to concede the virtues of individuality, the breaking-down of the walls of isolation can sometimes become a means of encouraging minority groups to give up their identity; participation in a pluralistic democracy can become a way of creating one people with one culture. We praise pluralism, yet press for conformity. In our own country and in our world the problem is real and the stakes are high.

The recent Ecumenical Council, Vatican II, made pluralism a living issue for Judeo-Christian relations. Specifically, the suggestion that there be a continuing religious dialogue between the groups has caused controversy within the Jewish community, and has made a proper understanding of the encounter of different religions a vital necessity.

We sometimes forget that the two faiths have confronted each other before, and often. Ever since Christianity changed from a Jewish sect into a separate religion, communicants of both faiths have engaged in dialogues, although hardly in what is today's "ecumenical spirit." The conversations were not usually amicable exchanges aimed at mutual enlightenment but, rather, angry polemics, each side seeking to refute and discredit the other once and for all.

Such debates were especially prevalent in medieval Europe, where the Sages of the Jewish community were often summoned to participate in what the powerful Christian clerics imagined would be an easy contest for themselves. They expected that they would triumph and the despised Jews would be confirmed in their humiliation or, better yet, converted to the "true faith." The atmosphere at these disputations was partly like a carnival, partly like a Soviet Russian show trial. The Jewish disputants were in an impossible position. Should they lose, Judaism would be discredited and some Jews might be coaxed to the baptismal font. If they pressed their case too hard, they might arouse the fury of the authorities to let loose on them the ignorant and prejudiced mobs.

Occasionally, however, the authorities were less maleficent, more enlightened. When the Jewish leader was eminently knowledgeable, articulate, and fiercely independent while remaining circumspect, the polemic could become an extraordinary theological exploration. Such a combination of circumstances arose in thirteenth-century Spain. Pablo Christiani, a baptized Jew, incited his new co-religionists to order the Jews to debate on religion before the King. Unfortunately for Pablo, Rabbi Moses ben Nahman was chosen to be the representative of the Jews.

Nahmanides, as he is usually known, was the leading Jew of his time. Considered one of the most eminent Talmudists of all Jewish history, among the Sephardi Halakhic masters he is second only to Maimonides, with whom he often took issue. His commentaries on the Bible are studied assiduously to this day. A gifted and original mystic, he is identified by his choice as the Jewish representative in the debate in Barcelona as a significant communal leader. The passage which follows is taken from the account of the debate which Nahmanides reports having written immediately after its conclusion.

Why return, at this late date, to the bitter and acrimonious polemics of a benighted age? First, it is important to remember that Jewish-Christian confrontations have a history, and not always a pleasant one. While we should appreciate the far different spirit prevailing today, we cannot enter contemporary interconfessional dialogue ignorant of the intense differences of opinion discovered in such encounters in the past. Second, and more important, distasteful as these old clashes may seem, the very hostility involved made possible a measure of honesty often lacking in contemporary exchanges, in which participants sometimes feel inhibited about talking of crucial but tension-arousing matters. Third, such historical awareness may guide us to direct our attention, in interreligious consultations, to the social and economic problems that are our common lot, rather than to the area of theology, where our private spiritual commitments are often incommensurate.

THE DEBATE WITH PABLO CHRISTIANI
Nahmanides

In this selection two major fundamentals of Christianity, both denied by Judaism, are discussed: the Messiahship and divinity of Jesus. Pablo's major thrust, in keeping with the Christian theology of his time, is to prove the truth of the Christian witness from the Jewish sources, an extension of the Christian idea that Jesus is presaged in the Old Testament. Going a step further, Pablo argues that even post-Christian rabbinical sources imply the doctrines of Christianity, or at least prove their correctness.

Thus the Jewish-Christian argument, as formulated in the period under discussion, necessarily involves exegesis: the interpretation not only of Biblical verses but also of Talmudic and Midrashic passages. Several such exegetical contests appear in this selection. Even if the terms of reference are no longer particularly relevant for the confrontation of the two religions, they convey to the modern reader some flavor of the great disputations of the past. Moreover, they reveal both the seriousness with which the

members of both faiths took Scripture, and the intellectual vigor
they brought to their interpretive tasks.

2.

Our lord the King commanded me to debate with Friar Pablo
Christiani before the King and his counselors in his palace in Barcelona. I answered and said: I will do as my lord the King commands if you will permit me to speak as I wish. I ask permission
for this from the King and Friar Raymund of Penyaforte and his
colleagues who are present.

3.

Friar Raymund of Penyaforte answered: As long as you do not
speak insultingly.

4.

I said to them: I cannot engage in this disputation unless I am
permitted to speak as I wish on the subject of the debate, even as
you will speak freely as you wish. I have enough sense to speak
politely, but I must be able to say what I wish. And they gave me
permission to say what I wish; even the King did.

5.

And so I answered and said: The controversy between Gentiles
and Jews concerns many doctrines which are not of the essence of
religion. But in this honored court I wish to debate only matters
which are basic and on which all else depends.

6.

They all answered and said: You have spoken well. So we agreed
to speak first about whether the Messiah has already come, as the

Christians believe, or whether he will come in the future, as the Jews believe. Then we shall speak about whether the Messiah is actually God, or whether he is completely human, born of a man and a woman. Then we shall speak about whether the Jews or the Christians possess the true religion and proper faith.

Here follows a debate between Nahmanides and Pablo about whether the Messiah has already come. The argument now continues:

46.

Pablo arose and said: I will bring yet another proof that the time of the Messiah has already passed.

47.

Said I: My lord the King, hear me: the law and truth and justice of Judaism do not fundamentally depend upon Messiah; for you are worth more to me than the Messiah. You are a king, and he —the Messiah—is a king. You are a Gentile king, and he is a Jewish king, for the Messiah is but a flesh-and-blood king even as you are. Now when I serve my Creator in your domain, in exile and in persecution and in subjection, constantly reviled by Gentiles, my reward is very great; for I make of myself a complete offering to God, and thereby I am all the more deserving of the life of the world-to-come. But when a Jewish king, of my faith, will rule over the nations, and I will perforce have to observe the Jewish religion, my reward will not be as great. So that the major point of contention between Jews and Christians is not this, but rather that you entertain a fundamental belief about God which we consider bitterly objectionable. You, our lord the King, are a Christian, the son of a Christian, and all your life you have listened to priests who have talked of the birth of Jesus, and have filled your mind and the very marrow of your bones with this story, until you have accepted it out of habit. But this belief of yours—and it is the foundation of your creed—is something that reason cannot accept, that goes against nature, and that the Prophets never said. It is even beyond miracles, as I shall explain with complete proofs at the proper time and place, that the Creator of Heaven and earth should turn into a fetus in the womb of a certain Jewess, develop there for nine months, be born as an infant, then grow up and fall into the hands of his enemies, be condemned to die and executed and then, as you say, be resurrected and return to what he originally was. The mind of a Jew, or any other human being, cannot accept such a thing. In vain do you speak to us of such things, for this is indeed what principally divides us. However, let us speak as well concerning the Messiah, if that is what you wish.

48.

Said Pablo: Do you believe that he has come?

49.

I said: No. Rather, I believe and I know that he has *not* come. Except for Jesus, no one has ever said of himself, nor had it said of him, that he is the Messiah. It is impossible for me to believe in his Messiahship, for the Prophet said of the Messiah, "He shall have dominion also from sea to sea, and from the river unto the ends of the earth" (Psalm 72:8), whereas he, Jesus, had no dominion at all. On the contrary, during his lifetime he was pursued by his enemies and forced to hide from them, and ultimately fell into their hands and was unable to save himself. How, then, shall he be considered the savior of Israel? Even after his death he had no special dominion, for the Roman Empire did not come about because of him. Before it adopted Christianity, Rome already ruled over most of the world. In fact, after they adopted belief in him, they began to lose many of their possessions. At the present time the Moslems, your enemies, have greater dominion than you. Thus too, the Prophet says that in the time of the Messiah, "No longer shall every man teach his neighbor and every man his brother saying, 'Know the Lord,' for they shall all know Me, from the least of them unto the greatest of them, says the Lord" (Jeremiah 31:34); moreover, "for the earth shall be full of the knowledge of the Lord as the waters cover the sea" (Isaiah 11:9); and "they shall beat their swords into plowshares, and their spears into pruning-hooks; nation shall not lift up sword against nation, neither shall they learn war any more" (ibid., 2:4). But from the days of Jesus until this very day, the whole world is full of violence and oppression, the Christians spilling more blood than any others, and they are also immoral. How difficult would it be for you, my lord the King, and for your generals if you should "not learn war any more"! Furthermore, the Prophet says of the Messiah, "and he shall smite the land with the rod of his mouth" (ibid., 11:4). The Sages explain this verse, in the text of the Midrash which Pablo has in his hand, as follows: when it will be told to the King Messiah, "such and such a state is rebelling against you," he will say, "let the locust come and destroy it"; if they will say, "such and such a district is rebelling against you," he will say, "let the wild beasts come and destroy it" (Midrash on Psalms 2). Thus he will rule "by the rod of his mouth" rather than by military means. Now this did not occur with Jesus. You, who worship him, prefer armored cavalry, and sometimes even all this does not help you. In addition to this, I can bring you yet many more proofs from the words of the Prophets.

50.

That man cried out and said: Again, as always, he makes long speeches, when there is something I want to ask.

51.

The King said to me: Keep silent, for he shall now ask. And I kept silent.

52.

Pablo said: Their Sages said concerning the Messiah that he is more honored than the angels. Now this is impossible save for Jesus, for he is both the Messiah and God Himself, and he carried out what was said in the Aggadah:

"Behold my servant shall prosper, he shall be exalted and lifted up and shall be very high" (Isaiah 52:13). "Shall be exalted"—more than Abraham; "and lifted up"—more than Moses; "and shall be very high"—more than the ministering angels (Yalkut to Isaiah, 476).

53.

Said I to him: Our Sages always say this concerning *all* the righteous; thus: "the righteous are greater even than the ministering angels" (*Sanhedrin* 93a). Similarly, according to the Sages, our teacher Moses said to the angel: "In the place where I sit you arc not permitted to stand" (Sifre, *Nitzavim* 308). Concerning the congregation of Israel, they said: "Israel is more beloved than the ministering angels" (*Hullin* 91b). What the author of this Aggadah meant to say about the Messiah is this: Abraham proselytized amongst the pagans and preached to them the belief in God, and he fought against Nimrod and was not afraid of him. Moses went even further; despite his humility he stood up to the great and wicked king Pharaoh, showed him no respect in the great plagues he brought upon him, and took Israel out of his land. Now the ministering angels are very energetic concerning the redemption of Israel, as it is written, "and there is none that sides with me against these, except Michael your prince" (Daniel 10:21); and similarly, "and now I will return to fight with the prince of Persia" (*ibid.,* v.20). But the Messiah will accomplish more than all of them: "And his heart was lifted up in the ways of the Lord" (II Chronicles 17:6). He will come to tell the Pope and all the kings of the nations in the Name of God, "Let My people go that they may serve Me" (Exodus 8:17). He shall perform many great wonders and miracles and shall not be afraid of them at all; he shall stand in the midst of their city Rome until he destroys it. I can proceed to explain the entire matter if you wish.

But he did not so wish.

72.

On the third day after this, our lord the King designated his palace as the place of the disputation, and ordered that it be held privately. We sat at the entrance to the palace. Pablo began with foolish words of no consequence, and then he said: I shall bring proof from one of their great Sages, such that there was none like him for the past four hundred years: Rabbi Moses the Egyptian (Maimonides). He says that the Messiah will die, and that his son and then his grandson will reign after him. If that is so, then it cannot be, as you have said, that he will live for ever. He then asked that the "Book of Judges," of Maimonides' *Mishneh Torah,* be brought to him.

73.

I said to them: That book does not contain such a passage. [Maimonides does say so elsewhere—in his Epistle on Resurrection, Chapter 6.] But I admit that there are some of our Sages who do believe that Messiah will live forever; as I said earlier, the opinion of some of the books of the Aggadah is that he was born on the day of the destruction of the Temple and will live forever. However, those who follow the plain and less fanciful meaning of our traditions are of the opinion that he will be born shortly before the appointed time of the redemption, will live many years, and will die amidst great honor, and bequeath his crown to his son. I have already stated that it is this second opinion which I accept, and that there is no difference, regarding such matters, between these days and the days of the Messiah save that Israel will no longer be under the domination of foreign powers.

74.

They then brought to him the book he had requested; he searched in it and did not find what he was looking for. I took the book from his hand and I said: Listen to the words of the book which he holds. I read to them from Maimonides, Book of Judges, Laws of Kings, beginning of Chapter 11: "King Messiah will arise for Israel, rebuild the Sanctuary, and gather the dispersed of Israel."

75.

Friar Arnold de Segarra said: He (Maimonides) lies!

76.

I said: Until now you considered him a Sage, of unparalleled greatness, and now you say he lies?

77.

At which the King scolded him and said: It is not proper to insult wise men.

78.

I said to the King: He does not lie, and I shall prove from the Pentateuch and from the Prophets that all that he says is the truth: that the task of Messiah is to gather the dispersed of Israel, and the exiles of Judah, all twelve tribes. Your Messiah, Jesus, did not gather in a single man, and did not even live during the Dispersion. The Messiah is responsible for the rebuilding of the Sanctuary and Jerusalem, whereas Jesus neither built nor destroyed anything. The Messiah will reign over the nations, whereas Jesus did not succeed even in protecting himself. I then read to them passages from Scripture which deal with the redemption to come, the portion beginning with "It shall be when all these things are come upon you, the blessing and the curse . . ." (Deuteronomy 30:1) until "And the Lord your God will put all these curses upon your enemies, and on them that hate you, that persecuted you (*ibid.,* v.7). I explained to them that "your enemies" refers to the Christians, and "them that hate you" to the Moslems, for it is these two peoples who have persecuted us. They answered nought to this, and they departed.

79.

The next day, the fourth, arrangements were made for the disputation to take place in the palace. The King, as usual, sat on his throne against the wall. The Bishop was there, together with many princes and leaders of the Church, noblemen, ordinary townsfolk, and many of the poor masses.

80.

I said to the King: I do not wish to continue the debate.

81.

Said the King: But why?

82.

I said: There is a great crowd here, and they have all pleaded with me to refrain from engaging in this debate, for they are afraid of the preachers who spread fear over everyone. Some of the greatest and most distinguished of the priests have sent word to me asking me not to continue. Many of the noblemen of your own household, my lord the King, have said to me that it is wrong for me to speak out against their religion in front of them. Even Friar Peter de Janua, the Sage of the Franciscans, has told me that it is not good. Also, some of the ordinary people have said to a number of Jews that I should not continue. And indeed so it was; this was their opinion. But when they saw that the King willed otherwise, they hemmed and hawed and said that I should continue. So the King and I discussed it at some length. The conclusion was that he told me to continue the debate. But, said I, it is only right that for one day I should do the asking and Pablo the answering, because for three days he has been doing the questioning and I the answering.

83.

Said the King: Nevertheless, answer his questions. I conceded.

84.

Pablo arose and asked: Do you believe that the Messiah of whom the Prophets spoke will be completely human, a man born of a man and a woman, or actually God?

85.

I said: From the very beginning we agreed that we would first speak about whether Messiah already came, as you maintain, and that afterward we would talk about whether he is God Himself. Now, you have not proved that he came, for I have disproven all the empty arguments which you brought. Thus I have won the debate, because, as you acknowledged at the outset, the burden of proof is upon you. If you still do not concede that I have won, I am prepared to bring completely convincing proofs, if you are willing to listen to me. But if it is clear that your Jesus is not the Messiah, then there is no point in debating whether our Messiah who is yet to come in the future will be completely human or what have you.

86.

The wise men among the judges who were present declared that I was right.

87.

The King said to me: Nevertheless, answer!

88.

I said: The truth is that the Messiah will come, and that he will be completely human, the product of relations between a man and a woman, even as I am. He will be a descendant of David, as it is written, "There shall come forth a shoot out of the stock of Jesse," the father of David (Isaiah 11:1). Thus too is it written, "The scepter shall not depart from Judah, nor the ruler's staff from between his feet, until Shiloh will come" (Genesis 49:10), referring to Messiah's descent from David, who himself is descended from Judah. For *Shiloh* means "his son," deriving from the word *shiliah*, which means "the afterbirth." Now were he the spirit of God, as you say, he could not be considered to be of "the stock of Jesse." And even if he had tarried in the womb of a woman who herself was descended from Jesse, i.e., David, he could not be considered the heir to his throne, for according to the law of the Torah, daughters and their progeny do not inherit where there are sons, and in every generation there were male descendants of David.

89.

He said: In the Psalms (110:1) we read, "A Psalm of David: The Lord saith unto my lord: 'Sit thou at My right hand, until I make thine enemies thy footstool.' " Now to whom, other than to God, would King David say "my lord"? And how can a mere man sit at the right hand of God? Obviously, then, it must refer to the Messiah who is also God—i.e., Jesus.

90.

Said the King: He asks well! Were the Messiah completely human and actually from the seed of David, David would never address him as "my lord." If I had a son or a grandson, my own seed, even if he ruled over the whole world, I would never call him "my lord." Rather, I would want him to address me as "my lord" and to kiss my hand.

91.

I turned my face to Pablo and I said to him: So you are the brilliant Jew who has made this great discovery, was baptized because of it, and told the King to assemble for you the Sages of the Jews in order to debate with them concerning these original ideas which you have discovered! Do you think we have never heard this before? There is neither priest nor child who does not ask the same question of the Jews! It is indeed quite an old question.

92.

Said the King: But answer it.

93.

I said: Hear me out now. King David was the poet who composed these Psalms, under the influence of the holy spirit, that they be sung before the altar of the Lord. He himself did not sing them; indeed, he was forbidden to do so by the law of the Torah, and that is why he gave them to the Levites for them to sing. Thus it is written explicitly in the Book of Chronicles (I, 16:7). Hence he had to write the Psalms in language appropriate for the Levite. Had he, then, written "The Lord saith unto *me:* Sit at My right hand," he would have caused the Levite to utter an untruth—for the Lord said nothing of the sort to the Levite! But it is perfectly in order for the Levite to recite, in the Temple, the words, "The Lord saith unto *my lord*—meaning David—sit at My right hand." This expression, "sit at My right hand," means that God will defend him and protect him and make him victorious over his enemies. Indeed, this came to pass; for David slew eight hundred of his enemy at one time (II Samuel 23:8, 18). Are there any among your warriors here who can lay claim to such feats? This is what is meant by "the right hand" of God. Thus we find this figure of speech elsewhere: David himself writes, "Your right hand has held me up" (Psalm 18:36), and "The right hand of the Lord does valiantly; the right hand of the Lord is exalted" (Psalm 118:15, 16); concerning Moses it is written, "That caused His glorious arm to go at the right hand of Moses" (Isaiah 63:12), and concerning the defeat of Pharaoh, "Your right hand, O Lord, dashes the enemy in pieces" (Exodus 15:6).

Besides all this, it is Biblical style to use the third person for the first person. Thus Samuel recounts the history of Israel to the people and says, "And the Lord sent Jerubbaal and Bedan and Jephthah and Samuel" (I Samuel 12:11), instead of ". . . and Jephthah and me." Or, Lamech refers to his wives as "Ye wives of Lamech" (Genesis 4:23) instead of "my wives." Similarly, the entire Torah is written by Moses, yet he refers to himself in the third person. Here too, then, David refers to himself in the third person: not as "the Lord saith unto me," but "the Lord saith unto my lord." This is in addition to the fact that he was forced to use this expression, as I have mentioned before, because it was composed for others to recite.

Furthermore, these Psalms were written under the influence of the holy spirit. They therefore refer not only to David himself but also to his son who would sit on his throne—by that I mean the Messiah—for what was only partially true for David will reach its completion with the Messiah his descendant. Thus, "the right hand" of the Holy One will support David himself until he vanquishes his immediate enemies that surround him. It will help the

Messiah until He makes of all the nations the Messiah's "footstool," for they are all his enemies, in that they have enslaved his people and denied his coming and his kingdom. Some of these nations have even proclaimed another as the Messiah. It is thus appropriate to chant this Psalm in the Temple both in the days of David and in the days of Messiah his son, for this Psalm was meant both for David and for his descendants after him.

94.

Pablo answered: How can he say that? Their Sages say that the Psalm speaks of the Messiah, and that the words are to be taken literally—that he, the Messiah, will sit at God's right hand. And he then cited the Aggadah (Yalkut to Psalms, 869) which relates that in the future the Holy One will seat Messiah at His right and Abraham at His left.

95.

I said: This too is as I said, for I maintained that the Psalm refers partly to David, but in its fullest sense to the Messiah. I then asked for the book containing the Aggadah, and they gave it to me.

96.

I then continued: See how Pablo deceives! For this Aggadah states that in the time to come the Holy One will seat Messiah to His right and Abraham to His left, and Abraham's face will grow pale and he will say, "The son of my son sits to the right of the Holy One, whereas I sit only to the left of Him!" The Holy One will then appease him, saying, "The son of your son sits to the right, and so am I at your right hand." Now from this you have explicit proof that the Messiah is not God, and that Jesus is not at all the Messiah; for were the Messiah God, Abraham would not be ashamed because God is more honored than he, and his face would not grow pale. Thus, too, he refers to Messiah as "the son of my son" and not as "the son of my daughter"—whereas Jesus, according to your story, is not at all the "son of the son" of Abraham. The Messiah's sitting to the right, like Abraham's sitting to the left, is an indication of the complete humanity of both. Thus, too, does this prove that Jesus is not the Messiah, for the Aggadah speaks of the time-to-come, the future, and the Sages who are the authors of this passage lived some five hundred years after Jesus. But Pablo wants to have it both ways, and isn't even embarrassed by this deception.

97.

He then continued and brought proof from the Midrash (Yalkut to *Behukotai,* 672) on the verse in which the Lord says to Israel, "And I will walk among you" (Leviticus 26:12). The Midrash presents a parable:

To what may this be compared? To a King who went for a walk in his orchard with his tenant-farmer, and the latter was so frightened that he hid from the King. Said the King to him: "Why do you hide from me? I am just like you!" So in the future, the Holy One will walk with the righteous in the Garden of Eden, and when the righteous will see Him, they will tremble. The Holy One will then say to them, "Why do you tremble before Me?—I am just like one of you!" You might think that therefore there is no need at all for the fear of God? Therefore it is written, "And I will be your God and ye shall be My people."

Now since God says to them "I am just like one of you," therefore He becomes a man just like them.

98.

I said: If Pablo understood, he would realize that his "proofs" disprove him! For this story is told of what will be in the future, in the Garden of Eden; and Jesus never walked with the righteous in the Garden of Eden during his lifetime, but fled from his enemies and pursuers all his days. But actually this Midrash is not meant to be taken literally, for it is a parable. Thus indeed the passage begins with: "To what can this be compared?" What it means is that the righteous of this world cannot attain the full truth of prophecy. They cannot behold what is known as the "glory" of God, as it is written, "If there be a prophet among you, I the Lord do make Myself known unto him in a vision, I do speak with him in a dream" (Numbers 12:6). The communication is by a dim vision or dream, but not a perception of the glory of God directly. Even our teacher Moses, at the beginning of his prophetic ministry, trembled: "And Moses hid his face for he was afraid to look upon God" (Exodus 3:6). But in the time to come, the souls of the righteous will be purified of all sin and pollution, and they will be permitted to gaze upon the "luminous mirror," the very glory of God, even as was later true of Moses concerning whom it is written, "The Lord spoke to Moses face to face, as a man speaks to his friend" (Exodus 33:11). Thus the words "I am just like one of you" is a figure of speech, a metaphoric assurance that the righteous need not tremble and fear, even as they are not afraid one of the other. This is no different from the language of Scripture which we just cited that God spoke to Moses "as a man speaks to his friend," which certainly does not mean that God became a man when He spoke to Moses! It is a matter of Rabbinic style too, such as the statement in the Midrash Yelamdenu, "If you will perform My commandments, then you shall be like Me." So again, in Biblical style: "Ye shall be as God, knowing good and evil" (Genesis 3:5); or, "The Lord God said, behold the man is become as one of us" (ibid., v.22); or, "He that stumbleth among them on that day shall be as David, and the house of David shall be as God" (Zechariah 12:8). In all these cases no equality or identity is implied.

99.

Then that man continued, and argued from the Midrash Rabbah (Genesis Rabbah 2:5) that the "spirit of God" in the verse "and the spirit of God hovered over the face of the waters" (Genesis 1:2) refers to the spirit of the Messiah. Thus, he concluded, Messiah is not a man but the spirit of God.

100.

I said: Woe to one who knows nothing, yet thinks he is wise and learned! For that same Midrash says that "the spirit of God" which hovered refers to the spirit of Adam; does that mean that he was a God? One who cannot find his way in the sacred books distorts the words of the Living God!

The Sage who comments that "the spirit of God" refers to "the spirit of Messiah" interprets all these Biblical verses as relating to various kingdoms, and as alluding to future events. Thus:

"The earth was unformed" refers to Babylon, as in "I beheld the earth (Babylon) and lo, it was unformed" (Jeremiah 4:23); "void" refers to Media, as in "they hastened (va-yavhilu) to bring Haman" (Esther 6:14)—va-yavhilu derives from behalah, which is the same as bohu, void, and Haman was of Media; "darkness" refers to Greece, which darkened the light of Israel by their evil decrees; "the face of the deep" refers to the Evil Kingdom, for evil is as impenetrable as the deep; and "the spirit of God" refers to the spirit of Messiah. By what merit does this spirit of Messiah "hover over the face of the waters"? —by virtue of repentance, which has been compared to water ("Pour out thy heart like water"—Lamentations 2:19).

Now this Midrash enumerates four kingdoms, the last of which —the Evil Kingdom—refers to Rome, after which He will bring "the spirit of God," which is Messiah: one completely human, but filled with wisdom and the spirit of God, even as was Bezalel, of whom it was said, "I have filled him with the spirit of God, in wisdom . . ." (Exodus 31:3), and also Joshua, of whom it was said, "Joshua the son of Nun was full of the spirit of wisdom" (Deuteronomy 34:9). It is thus clear that the Sages here speak of Messiah, who will come after the fourth kingdom.

I could not tell them any more about the contents of this Midrash, because it contains allusions and hints based upon similarities in language of the various words of Scripture rather than upon its major content. This is true of many passages in Genesis Rabbah, such as its interpretation of "And Jacob went out" (Genesis 28:10) as alluding to the four kingdoms in which Israel suffered exile. I said to them what I did in order to show all of them that Pablo was unable to read the book he intended to use as support, and that he erred in reading the very words.

101.

The King arose, and so did they all arise.

102.

This is the record of all the debates. I have not, to my knowledge, changed a single word. Afterward, that very day, I appeared before our lord the King, and he said, "Let the debate stop here, for I have never seen a man who is in the wrong who can argue his case as well as you did." I heard in the court that the King and the preachers wanted to appear in the synagogue on the Sabbath. I remained in the city another eight days. When they came on the Sabbath, I answered our lord the King properly, for he persisted in preaching that Jesus is the Messiah.

103.

I then got up on my feet and I said: I consider the words of our lord the King as noble and excellent and honored; for they issue from the mouth of one who is himself noble and excellent and honored above all others in the world. But I shall not praise them by declaring them to be true. For I have unimpeachable proofs and words as clear as sunshine that show that the truth is not as he says; but it is not proper to dispute him. But there is one thing

I must mention for it astonishes me greatly. The King's words urging us to believe that Jesus is the Messiah were presented to our ancestors by Jesus himself. It was he who endeavored to convince them of this. Yet they strongly and completely rejected it. He certainly knew and was able to verify his claims more than the King, especially according to your belief that he is God. Now if our ancestors, who saw him and knew him personally, did not accept him, how shall we believe in him? Shall we now accept the opinion of the King who knows nothing of the matter except from a long chain of reports coming from people who did not know him and did not come from the same country as did our ancestors who knew him and were present at the time?

104.

After this Friar Raymund of Penyaforte arose and preached concerning the trinity, and said that it consists of God's wisdom and will and power. And he said in the synagogue: also the Rabbi (Nahmanides) admitted this to Pablo in Gerona at a previous debate.

105.

I stood up on my feet and I said: Listen to me carefully, Jews and Gentiles. Pablo asked me in Gerona if I believe in the trinity. I said to him: What do you mean by trinity—that the divinity consists of three crude bodies, such as humans? No, he said. That it consists of three spiritual elements such as souls, or three angels? He said: No. Or that it means one item composed of three others, such as the body which is composed of the four elements? He said: No. What then do you mean by the trinity? He said: (God's) wisdom, will, and power. I said to him that I admit that God is wise and not ignorant, that He wills without experiencing emotion, that He is powerful and not weak. But the term "three" is completely erroneous, for wisdom in the Creator is not an acci-

dent, that is, superadded to and separate from Him such that it is
conceivable for Him not to be wise. Rather, He and His wisdom
are One, He and His will are One, He and His power are One.
And even were we to consider them accidents, unessential to Him,
it does not mean that God is three but that He is One who possesses these three accidents. Our lord the King has here repeated a
simile that those who err have taught him, namely, that the Divinity is like wine which has three qualities, color, taste, and odor,
and yet remains one. But this is totally mistaken, for redness and
taste and odor in wine are separate from each other, for one can
exist without the other. There is red and white and other colors.
So too may one say about taste and odor. Further, it is neither the
redness nor the taste nor the odor which constitutes the wine; that
which fills the vessel is the wine itself. It is therefore a substance
which possesses three distinct accidents which are not one. And if,
by error, we are going to enumerate accidents as substances, then
we must conclude that God is not a trinity but a quaternity, for
you must count God plus His wisdom and will and power, which
makes four. Even more, you ought to believe in a quinary, for He
is also alive, and life should be mentioned as is wisdom; thus you
would have life, wisdom, will, power, and God Himself. All this is
obviously erroneous.

106.

Then Pablo arose and declared that he believed in complete Unity
but that nevertheless He consists of three, but that this is a subject
that is very profound such that even the angels and the Princes of
Heaven do not understand it.

107.

I arose and I said: It is obvious that a person does not believe that
which he does not know. Therefore the angels do not believe in
the trinity. At this, Pablo's colleagues bade him keep silent.

108.

Then our lord the King arose and all descended from the pulpit and left. The next day I presented myself before our lord the King and he said to me: Return to your city to life and peace. He gave me three thousand dinarii for my travel expenses and I took my leave of him in great love. May God grant me the privilege of life in the world to come, Amen.

18. Nature*

In the Jewish view man has certain duties and responsibilities toward his natural environment. It was given to him in trust, not outright, and therefore he must answer to God for his conduct toward it. "The earth is the Lord's" (Psalm 24:1).

The establishment and maintenance of a good society must therefore take into account the manner in which man disports himself in nature—how he behaves vis-à-vis the streams and forests, the air and the trees.

It is only recently that such concerns have come to public attention all over the world. While formerly only "conservationists" dealt with these issues, their warnings have suddenly taken on new meaning. "Ecology" is now a universally major concern: unless men change their ways immediately, we are bound to suffer irrevocably from our thoughtless abuse and exploitation of nature.

In truth, these issues of ecology are new only in their urgency. The result of technological breakthroughs since the Industrial Revolution, the principles were already well known in ages gone by.

The Bible, Halakhah, and Jewish philosophy have always

* Much of this material is adapted from a chapter in my *Faith and Doubt: Studies in Traditional Jewish Thought* (New York: Ktav, 1971).

sought to guide man on how to set up a good society that is respectful of its natural setting. Harmony with nature and peace in society are based on respect for the natural world. The relation of such respect to man's spiritual and moral life is best exemplified by the Rabbis:

> By ten divine utterances was the world created.
> Why does the Torah indicate this? Surely the world could have been created by one divine utterance!
> It comes to tell us that God will exact severe penalty from the wicked who destroy the world which was created by no less than ten utterances, and that He will grant rich reward to the righteous who maintain the world was created by ten utterances. (*Ethics of the Fathers* 5:1.)

Biblical and Talmudic Perspectives

The starting point for a religious consideration of man's relations with his natural environment is the divine blessing to man in Genesis 1:28: ". . . be fruitful and multiply and replenish the earth and subdue it; and have dominion over the fish of the sea and over the fowl of the air and over every creeping thing that creeps on the earth."

The above passage, mandating man's conquest of nature, has recently come under attack by those concerned with protecting natural resources and environment from the excesses and abuses of man. Some theologians have even seen in this verse sanction for man's mindless rape of nature and an impediment to the search for knowledge and the advancement of science.

This charge, particularly as it is refuted by an analysis of the manner in which the same Biblical verse is interpreted in the tradition, is an empty one. The Torah's respect for non-human nature is evident in the restrictions that follow immediately upon the "subdue" commandment: man is permitted only to *eat* herbs and greens, not to abuse the resources of nature (Genesis 1:29). Furthermore, this mastery over nature is limited to vegetables for the first ten generations. Vegetarianism yields to carnivorousness only after the Flood when, as a concession, God permits the eating of meat by the sons of Noah. Even then, the right to devour flesh is circumscribed with a number of protective prohibitions, such as the warnings against eating blood and taking human life (Genesis 9:2–6). The law of *kashrut* preserves the kernel of that primeval vegetarianism by placing selective restrictions on man's appetite for meat. His right to "subdue" nature is by no means unlimited.

Man and Earth

Man's commanding role in the world brings with it a commensurate responsibility for the natural order. Adam is punished for his sin by the diminution of nature's potencies: thorns and thistles, sweat of the brow, enmity between the species, complications in the relations between the sexes, the ultimate victory of earth over man (Genesis 3:15–19). Upsetting the balance of nature, man included, becomes a curse. Cain, too, is punished by alienation from nature. The blood of his slain brother is soaked up by the earth, corrupting it and disturbing its peace, and the retribution is in kind: "When you till the ground, it shall not henceforth yield you its strength; a fugitive and wanderer shall you be in the earth" (Genesis 3:4–12). Ten generations later the world is filled with "violence" (*hamas*), "for all flesh has corrupted their way on the earth," and, hence, "behold, I will destroy them with the earth" (Genesis 6:11–12). And in the eschatological vision of Isaiah, the restoration of man to primordial harmony in and with nature is the Prophet's most powerful metaphor for the felicity of the Messianic redemption. "And the wolf shall dwell with the lamb . . . and a little child shall lead them. . . . They shall not hurt nor destroy in all My holy mountain" (Isaiah 11:6–9).

Biblical concern for the ecological balance in territory from which a large population had been banished because of warfare is evidenced when the Israelites are told of their eventual inheritance of Canaan from its original inhabitants: "I will not drive them out from before you in one year, lest the land become desolate, and the beasts of the field multiply against you. Little by little will I drive them out from before you, until you have increased and inherit the land" (Exodus 23:29–30). We find Biblical legislation to enforce pollution abatement in the commandment to dispose of sewage and waste by burial in the ground rather than by dumping into streams or littering the countryside (Deuteronomy 23:13–15).

Perhaps the most powerful expression of concern for man's respect for the integrity of nature as the possession of its Creator, rather than his own preserve, is the Sabbath. This institution, never solely a matter of rest and refreshment, pointed primarily to the relationships between man, world, and God. The six workdays were given to man in which to carry out the commission to "subdue" the world, to impose on nature his creative talents. But the seventh day is a Sabbath; man must cease his creative interference in the natural order (the Halakhah's definition of *melakhah,* or work) and by this act of renunciation demonstrate his awareness that the earth is the Lord's. The same principle underlies the institutions of the Sabbatical and Jubilee years. The Sages of the Mishnah interpreted "a song for the Sabbath day" (Psalm 92) as "a song for the hereafter, for the day which will be all Sabbath." For the Rabbis the weekly renunciation of man's role as interloper and manipulator, and his symbolic gesture of regard for nature, was thus extended into a perpetual Sabbath.

The Orders of Creation

This respect for the inviolability of nature takes in its major segments as well. The original identity of species must be protected against artificial distortion and obliteration. This confirmation of the separateness and noninterchangeability of its various parts may be said to lie at the heart of some of the less rationally appreciated (Pentateuchal commandments—those prohibiting the mixing of different seeds in a field, of interbreeding diverse species of animals, of wearing garments of mixed wool and linen. Here the Bible demands a symbolic affirmation of nature's original order in defiance of man's manipulative interference, threatening entire species with extinction.

Interestingly, one of the major Biblical sources of the laws forbidding such intermingling of species is immediately preceded by the famous commandment, "You shall love your neighbor as yourself" (Leviticus 19:18). Reverence for the integrity of identity is common to both laws. Respect for the wholeness of a fellow man's autonomy must lead to respect for the wholeness of all the Creator's works, nature included. This autonomy of nature is known in rabbinical literature as *sidrei bereshit,* the "orders of creation." The rabbinical attitude to these "orders of creation" is manifest in the following passage:

Our Rabbis taught: once there was a man whose wife died and left him with a nursing child. He had no money to pay a wet-nurse. A miracle happened, and he developed two breasts like a woman and he nursed his child. Said R. Joseph: "Come and see, how great is this man that such a miracle should have been performed for him." Said Abaye to him: "On the contrary, how lowly is this man that for his sake the orders of creation should have been altered."

You Shall Not Destroy

The Biblical norm which most directly addresses itself to the ecological situation is that known as *bal tashhit,* "you shall not destroy."

When you besiege a city a long time, in making war against it to take it, you shall not destroy the trees thereof by wielding an axe against them; for you may eat of them, but you shall not cut them down; for is the tree of the field man that it should be besieged by you? Only the trees of which you know that they are not trees for food, them you may destroy and cut down, that you may build bulwarks against the city that makes war against you until it fall (Deuteronomy 20:19–20).

These two verses admit of a variety of interpretations. But this much is obvious, that the Torah forbids wanton destruction. Vandalism against nature entails the violation of a Biblical prohibition. According to one medieval authority, the purpose of the commandment is to train man to love the good by abstaining from all destructiveness. "For this is the way of the pious . . . they love peace, are happy when they can do good to others and bring them close to Torah, and will not cause even a grain of mustard to be lost from the world. . . ."

The Talmudic and Midrashic traditions continue this implicit assumption of man's obligation to, and responsibility for, nature's integrity.

While the Biblical commandment of *bal tashhit* appears to cover only acts of vandalism performed during wartime, the Halakhah considers the law to cover all situations, in peacetime as well as in war. Indeed, while Maimonides forbids the destruction of fruit trees for use in warfare, other authorities, such as Rashi and Nahmanides, specifically exempt from the prohibition the use of fruit trees for such purposes as bulwarks; what is proscribed is not the use of trees to win a battle, which may often be a matter of life and death, but the wanton devastation of embattled areas so as to render them useless to the enemy should he win—in other words, a "scorched-earth" policy.

Nor is destroying by "wielding an axe" taken by the Halakhah as the exclusive means of destruction. Any form of despoliation is forbidden by Biblical law—even diverting the irrigation without which a tree will wither and die. As in its extension of the law from war to peacetime, the Halakhah assumed that the Torah was enunciating a general principle in the form of a specific and extreme case.

Similarly, the mention of "fruit trees" was expanded to include almost everything else. Thus, Maimonides: "And not only trees, but whoever breaks vessels, tears clothing, wrecks that which is built up, stops fountains, or wastes food in a destructive manner, transgresses the commandment of *bal tashhit,* but his punishment is only flogging by rabbinical edict." Likewise, is it forbidden to kill an animal needlessly or to offer exposed water (presumed to be polluted or poisoned) to livestock.

For the Talmud, *bal tashhit* was primarily a religio-moral injunction concerning economic value, rather than an economic law which has religious sanction. Thus, the seriousness with which the Talmud approaches this commandment, as is revealed in a story it tells of R. Hanina, who attributed the untimely death of his son to the latter's cutting down a fruit tree prematurely. The Rabbis hesitated to pay a sick call to a dying scholar who, for medical purposes, kept a goat in his house in order to drink its milk; goats despoil the grazing land and hence are to be banished from such pastures. The Tabernacle was built of acacia wood to teach man that if he wishes to build a house for himself he should not despoil fruit trees for this purpose. Even though one is Halakhically permitted to destroy a fruit tree if he wishes to build his home on its place, nevertheless he should refrain from doing so.

Judaism avoided the extreme of the deification and worship of nature on the one hand, and contempt for the world on the other. At the other pole, rabbinical Judaism, in the Mitnagdic version, completely and unequivocally denied to nature the dimension of holiness but conceded that from the divine perspective of reality ("from His side") there cannot be conceived a world not utterly suffused with the Presence. This theological tension is resolved, or at least committed to practice, with the aid of Halakhah: Nature is not to be considered holy, but neither is one permitted to act ruthlessly toward it, needlessly to ravage it and disturb its integrity.

Man as Creator

Within this framework, it is important to elaborate further on the relation of man to nature in order to provide the value foundation for the moral imperatives that issue from ecology. "And subdue it" certainly implies a mandate to man to exercise his technological talents and genius in the upbuilding of the world and the exploitation of nature's resources. From the days of R. Saadia Gaon and R. Sabbatai Donello, a thousand years ago, a tradition of interpretation has understood the Biblical term "the image of God" to include, if not primarily to signify, man's capacity for creativity. In a remarkable passage, of much earlier vintage, we read that Tyrannus Rufus, a pagan Roman general, asked R. Akiva which was more beautiful (or useful): the works of God or the works of man. Holding some stalks of grain in one hand, and loaves of bread in the other, R. Akiva showed the astounded pagan that the products of technology are more suited for man than the results of the natural process alone. So did R. Akiva proceed to explain the commandment of circumcision: world and man were created incomplete, God having left it to man to perfect his environment and his body. Similarly, the commandments, in general, were given in order that man thereby purify his character, that he attain spiritual perfection. Man must, in imitation of his Maker, apply his creative abilities to all life: his natural environment, his body, his soul.

When R. Shelomoh Eger, a distinguished Talmudist, became a Hasid, he was asked what he learned from R. Menahem Mendel of Kotzk after his first visit. He answered that the first thing he learned in Kotzk was, "In the beginning God created." But did a renowned scholar have to travel to a Hasidic Rebbe to learn the first verse in the Bible? He answered: "I learned that God created only the beginning; everything else is up to man."

However, this doctrine which teaches man's discontinuity with and superiority to the rest of the natural order must not be misconstrued as a sanction for man to despoil the world. First, while he is beyond the merely natural, he also participates in it; he is an intersection of the natural and the divine (or supernatural). The plurals in the verse, "And God said, Let *us* make man in *our* image," are explained by R. Joseph Kimhi as addressed by God to the earth, or nature. Man remains inextricably tied to nature while he is urged to transcend it. Man is a creature, and the denial of his creatureliness turns his creative powers to satanic and destructive ends.

Second, the very nature of the concept of the imagehood of man implies the warning that he must never overreach in arrogance. He may build, change, produce, create, but he does not hold title to the world, he is not the "King of the world," an appellation reserved exclusively for God. His subordinate role in the cosmic scheme means that nature was given to him to enjoy but not to ruin—a concept reinforced by the law that before deriving any benefit or pleasure from the natural world, such as eating or drinking, one must recite a blessing to the "King of the world," an acknowledgment that it is God and not man who holds ultimate title to the universe.

That man's role as co-creator with God must not be exaggerated we learn from the following Talmudic passage: "The rabbis taught: man was created on the eve of the Sabbath. Why? So that the Sadducees [i.e., heretics] should not say that God had a partner in the act of creation of the world." While man remains a partner of God in the ongoing creative process, we must distinguish between two Hebrew synonyms for creation: *beriah* and *yetzirah*. The former refers to creation out of nothing and hence can only be used of God. The latter describes creation out of some preexistent substance, and hence may be used of God (after the initial act of genesis) and of man. God has no "partners" in the onetime act of *beriah* with which He called the universe into being, and the world is, in an ultimate sense, exclusively His. He does invite man to join Him, as a co-creator, in the ongoing process of *yetzirah*. Hence, man receives from God the commission to "subdue" nature by means of his *yetzirah*-functions; but, because he is incapable of *beriah*, man remains responsible to the Creator for how he uses the world.

In the cosmic scene, God is the Owner, man the artisan, and the raw material is all the wealth of this world: nature, life, culture, society, intellect, family. Man is charged with applying to them his *yetzirah*-creative talents. He is commissioned to improve the world, build it up, transform it, "subdue" it. If he does so, he is "paid" for his labors. But man never has title over his own creations, he has no mastery over the world. Despite his investment of labor and talent, the world, even as perfected by man, belongs to the original Owner. No matter how extensive and ingenious man's scientific and technological achievements in the transformation, conquest, and improvement of nature, he cannot displace the rightful Owner who provided the material in the first place. And not only does man not have proprietorship over raw nature, but he is not even the absolute master of his own creations, the results of his magnificent *yetzirah*. He may not undo what he himself did, for once having done it, it belongs to the Owner and not to the artisan. Man must never entertain the notion that because he labored over his creations, he has the right to destroy them, to repeal his creativity. He remains a paid trustee over his very own products and must guard and watch over them with the greatest care.

Man the *yetzirah*-creator, according to the teaching of Halakhic Judaism, is responsible to God the *beriah*-Creator not only for the raw material of the natural world into which he was placed, but is responsible as well for protecting and enhancing the civilization which he himself created. "Subdue it" is not only not an invitation to ecological irresponsibility; it is a charge to assume additional moral responsibility not only for the natural world as such but even for the man-made culture and civilization which we found when we were born into this world.

Perhaps the most succinct summary of the role of man and nature is given early in the Biblical narrative of God's placing Adam in the Garden of Eden—which, from its description in Scripture, was a model of ecological well-being. "And the Lord God took the man and put him into the Garden of Eden to work it and watch over it" (Genesis 2:15). The undefiled world was given over to man "to work it," to apply to it his creative resources in order that it yield up to him its riches. But alongside the mandate to work and subdue it, he was appointed its watchman: to guard over it, to keep it safe, to protect it even from his own rapaciousness and greed. Man is not only an *oved,* a worker and fabricator; he is also a *shomer,* a trustee who, according to Halakhah, is obligated to keep the world whole for its true Owner.

19. Peace

Peace is not limited to political and international events alone. Its scope is far more extensive, including the harmony of society, community, family, and the inner life of man. Each of these stands under constant threat by various corrosive and disintegrating factors—from economic to psychological to spiritual—and "peace" is the challenge to preserve their integrity.

The Jewish ideal of peace, which is more than an absence of war, is contained in that overworked Hebrew word *shalom,* connoting wholeness, completeness, integrity, fulfillment, perfection. The masters of the Jewish tradition identified *shalom* as one of the Names of God. Indeed, in a manner of speaking, all of life is a search for and establishment of peace.

MIDRASH RABBAH
(*Naso 11:7*)

This passage is one of the greatest panegyrics to peace found in rabbinical literature. It is unusual not in tone or valuation but only in length and continuity of development. The section of the

Midrash Rabbah *to Numbers 6:26 expounds the last of the three verses comprising the* birkhat hakohonim, *the Priestly Benediction, heard in the liturgy: "The Lord bless you and keep you; the Lord make His face to shine upon you and be gracious unto you; the Lord lift up His countenance unto you and give you peace."*

The last part of the last line, "and give you peace," attracted the rabbinical commentators, who saw in it many meanings and recorded them in the Midrash. The Midrash Rabbah, *the Great Midrash, the one most studied and most often cited, is a collection of several volumes of interpretations of the five books of the Torah and the five Megillo read on the holidays. The ten volumes were compiled at widely different times, the earliest probably in the fourth century.*

The book from which this selection is taken, Numbers Rabbah, *is the last and was probably not compiled until about the twelfth century, at least in its present form. Nevertheless, most of the authorities cited here lived in the second and third centuries of the Common Era. Like all Midrashic commentaries on the Biblical texts, this book contains many opinions, some of which contradict others, with no attempt made to reconcile them.*

The treatment of shalom *in this passage is quite typical of Midrashic literature. Its statements are brief, ideas are quickly proposed, and the text moves on. Everything is done by reference to Biblical verses; the whole Bible thus becomes a commentary on the verse being expounded.*

Typically, the Rabbis did not confine themselves to one area or to a systematic treatment of peace. To them, "peace" included international accord, domestic tranquillity, spiritual integrity, and even personal serenity beyond the grave. (This passage contains the source of the expression used in speaking of the dead, "May he rest in peace.")

The passage also contains a number of special implications: first, the indirect assertion of the universality of peace, based on the concept that one nation cannot enjoy peace if it is denied to others. Second, the Midrash poses the conflict between the ideals of peace and truth. Which yields and which prevails? Is there a middle ground between "appeasing" and "warmongering"? Finally, note the remarkable practicality of the Midrashic Sages in

*their willingness to settle for as much of "peace" as is available:
even in the war there must be peace! Exactly what this means, and
its broader implications, the reader must ponder for himself.*

Great is peace, since for the sake of peace the Holy One altered
a statement. When He reported Sarah's statement to Abraham, He
quotes her as saying, "Indeed, shall I who am old bear a child?"
(Genesis 18:13), when in fact she had said, "My lord [Abraham]
being old" (*ibid.,* v.12). Thus, to preserve domestic peace,
God omitted Sarah's slight upon her husband.

Great is peace, as we see from the law concerning the wife accused by her husband of infidelity. In order to clear her from sus-
picion and thus restore peace between them, the Holy One commanded us to blot out with water His divine name which was
written on a scroll with all holiness, and thus make possible the
ordeal of the bitter waters as described in Numbers (5:23).

R. Eleazar says: Great is peace, for the prophets have taught
our people to care for nothing as much as for peace.

R. Simeon ben Halafta said: Great is peace, for no vessel holds
blessing so effectively as peace; as Scripture says, "The Lord will
bless His people with peace." Likewise, in the priestly benediction
God concludes with peace, *And Give You Peace.* This teaches
that other blessings in themselves are of no avail unless peace
goes with them.

R. Eleazar Hakkappar says: Great is peace, for the conclusion
of the whole of the Eighteen Benedictions is a prayer for peace,
and the conclusion of the priestly benediction is a prayer for
peace.

Great is peace, for it was given to the meek; as Scripture says,
"But the humble shall inherit the land, and delight themselves in
the abundance of peace" (Psalm 37:11).

Great is peace, for it outweighs everything else. We say in our
morning prayers: "He makes peace and creates everything": thus,
if there is no peace, there is, so to speak, nothing left in creation.

R. Eleazar, son of R. Eleazar Hakkappar, says that even if Israel serves idols, as long as peace reigns among them, the Holy
One, as it were, says about them: "My servant for punishment,

Satan, shall not touch them"; as Scripture says, "Ephraim is joined to idols; yet let him alone" (Hosea 9:17). But what does it say of Israel when they are in conflict? "Their heart is divided; now shall they bear their guilt" (Hosea 10:2). Thus, peace is a grand thing, and quarrelsomeness is hateful.

Peace is a grand thing, for even during war peace is necessary; as Scripture says, "When you draw near a city to fight against it, then proclaim peace unto it" (Deuteronomy 10:10). Scripture also says, "I sent messengers out of the wilderness of Kedemoth to Sihon . . . with words of peace" (Deuteronomy 2:26); and it says, "Restore those cities peaceably" (Judges 11:13).

Great is peace, for even the dying need peace; as Scripture says, "But you will go to your fathers in peace" (Genesis 15:15); and it says, "You shall die in peace" (Jeremiah 34:5).

Great is peace, for it was given to those who are repentant; as Scripture says, "Peace, peace, to him that is far off and to him that is near, says the Lord who creates the fruit of the lips" (Isaiah 57:19). Peace is thus granted to those who, though by their acts they previously removed themselves from God, now bring themselves near to Him and express their wrongs in confession.

R. Meir says: Great is peace, for the Holy One created no more desirable attribute than peace and it has been given to the righteous. When a righteous man departs from the world, three groups of ministering angels welcome him and each does so with a greeting of peace. The first says, "Let him enter into peace"; the second says, "Let them rest [peacefully] in their beds"; and the third says, "So it is for each one who walks in uprightness" (Isaiah 57:2).

Great is peace, for the Holy One, blessed be He, created no attribute more desirable than peace, and it has been withheld from the wicked. In the hour when a wicked man departs from the world, three groups of destroying demons confront him. The first says, "There is no peace." The second says, "Says the Lord concerning the wicked" (Isaiah 48:22). The third says, "You shall lie down in sorrow" (Isaiah 50:11).

Great is peace, for it was given as a reward for devotion to Torah and good deeds. As Scripture says, "If you walk in My statutes and keep My commandments" then the reward is "And I will establish peace in the land" (Leviticus 26:3, 6).

Great is peace, for it was given to those who love the Torah. As Scripture says, "Great peace have they that love Your law" (Psalm 119:165).

Great is peace, for it was given to those who study the Torah. As Scripture says, "All your children shall be taught by the Lord; and great shall be the peace of your children" (Isaiah 54:13).

Great is peace, for it was given to those who practice charity. As Scripture says, "The practice of charity shall mean peace" (Isaiah 32:17).

Great is peace, for God is called Peace. As Scripture says, "The angel said: The Lord is Peace" (Judges 6:24).

Great is peace, for even the angels in Heaven need peace, as Scripture says, "He makes peace in His high places" (Job 25:2). Now can we not reason from the less important to the more important? If peace is necessary in Heaven, a place where there is no hatred or enmity, how much more so is it necessary on earth, a place where all sorts of conflicts are found!

Observe now, said R. Simeon, that the way of the Holy One is not like the way of a mortal. If a mortal king goes to battle he goes accompanied by armies and legions, but when he goes on a peaceful mission he goes alone. That is not the way of the Holy One. When He goes on a mission of peace He goes forth with armies and with legions. As Scripture says, "He makes peace in His high Heavens," and after that it is written, "can His armies be numbered?" (Job 25:3). It also says, "The chariots of God are myriads, even thousands upon thousands; the Lord is among them in holiness as at Mt. Sinai" (Psalm 68:18). And Scripture says, concerning the revelation at Sinai, "Thousand thousands ministered unto him, and ten thousand times ten thousand" (Daniel 7:10). But when the Holy One goes to war, He goes entirely alone; as Scripture says, "The Lord is a man of war, the Lord is His Name" (Exodus 15:3). That teaches us that He fights by His Name alone and requires no aid. It also says, comparing wine to the blood of the battlefield, "I have trodden the winepress alone" (Isaiah 63:3). You find that when the Holy One inflicted punishment upon the evil Generation of the Flood, He did so entirely alone. As Scripture says, "I, even I, do bring the flood of waters" (Genesis 6:17).

Similarly, He punished the men of Sodom single-handed. As Scripture says, "Then the Lord brought a rain upon Sodom (*ibid.*, 19:24). The same was the case when He punished the Egyptians. As Scripture says, "The Lord smote all the firstborn" (Exodus 12:29). He likewise punished the Amorites single-handed. As Scripture says, "The Lord cast down great stones from Heaven upon them" (Joshua 10:11). He also punished Sennacherib single-handed. As Scripture says, "The angel of the Lord went forth, and smote the camp of the Assyrians" (II Kings 19:35). Is the case of an angel different? It is not, for an angel is an agent and a legal agent is, according to Jewish law, considered on a par with the principle.

Peace is a precious thing, since for all the deeds and meritorious acts which our father Abraham accomplished the greatest reward given him was peace. As Scripture says, "But you shall go to your fathers in peace" (Genesis 15:15). Likewise in the case of our father Jacob you find that he sought peace from God. As Scripture says, "So that I may come back to my father's house in peace" (*ibid.*, 28:21). So in the case of Aaron, and the priestly family descended from him, you find that he was praised by God mostly for peace. As Scripture says, "My covenant with him was one of life and peace" (Malachi 2:5).

You find likewise that the Torah was compared above all to peace. As Scripture says, "All her paths are peace" (Proverbs 3:17). Thus, you also find that the Holy One comforts Jerusalem, above all else, with the promise of peace. As Scripture says, "And My people shall abide in a peaceable habitation" (Isaiah 32:18). Similarly, He punished Ammon and Moab only by depriving them of peace. As Scripture says, "You shall not seek their peace nor their prosperity" (Deuteronomy 23:7). And Israel is blessed every day with peace. As Scripture says, *And Give You Peace*.

Further Reading

A. General Works

The themes covered in this book are so varied that it is difficult to recommend works which will cover most, or even many, of the individual subjects included. However, the following will offer valuable insights on the most important topics, as well as supplementary information on a number of literary genres selected.

Maimonides, from whose works a number of excerpts are included in this volume, is available to the English lay reader in a translation of some of the most important and relevant passages of his Code of Jewish Law. See Moses Maimonides, *Mishneh Torah;* Eng. trans. by Philip Birnbaum. (Bk. 1: Knowledge. "Ethical Ideas," pp. 11–22).) New York: Hebrew Publishing Co., 1967.

The Hafetz Hayyim (Chapter 5, on "Talebearing," is a translation of part of his most important writing) and his discourse on "kindness" are available in English as Israel Meir Kahana, *Ahavath hessed: kindness as required by God.* English trans. by Leonard Oschry. Jerusalem: Feldheim, 1967, pp. 77–231.

Insights into the ethical personalities of individual Jews may be gathered from Israel Abrahams, ed., *Hebrew Ethical Wills,* 2 vols., Philadelphia: Jewish Publications Society of America,

1926. A modern Jewish scholar who has written a concise and simple introduction to the social ethics of Judaism is Isidore Epstein, *The Jewish Way of Life,* London: E. Goldston, 1946. However, it is not easily available. Philip Birnbaum, whose edition of the *Mishneh Torah* is mentioned above, is the author of *A Book of Jewish Concepts,* New York: Hebrew Publishing Co., 1964. The entries in this concise, comprehensive, and readable one-volume encyclopedia range over the whole of Jewish life and literature; it is worth consulting for its information on many of the themes in this book. A volume which may be recommended for its discussion of social and moral ideas in Judaism is Meyer Waxman, *Judaism: Religion and Ethics,* New York: Yoseloff, 1958. (Part 2: "The Ethics of Judaism," pp. 203–390.) Solomon B. Freehof's two books on the Responsa Literature offer readable excepts from the entire range of this genre of "case histories" of Jewish Law—a number of which are included in the present volume—and also from leading rabbinical respondents touching on some of the issues raised here: *The Responsa Literature,* Philadelphia: JPSA, 1955, and *A Treasury of Responsa,* Philadelphia: JPSA, 1963. Finally, Louis Jacobs, a prolific Jewish scholar in England, has written three excellent volumes, all of which are readable, informative, and accurate, and which pay specific attention to the ethical and moral motifs of Judaism: *Jewish Values,* London: Vallentine, Mitchell, 1960; *Jewish Law,* New York: Behrman House, 1968; *Jewish Ethics, Philosophy, and Mysticism,* New York: Behrman House, 1969.

B. Selected Bibliography for Individual Chapters

Introduction: The various meanings of the term *hesed* are definitively presented in Nelson Glueck, *Hesed in the Bible.* Cincinnati: Hebrew Union College Press, 1967.

Chapter 1: What Is Required. For a readable and Halakhically profound treatment, see Samuel Belkin, *In His Image: the Jewish Philosophy of Man as Expressed in Rabbinic Tradition.* New York: Abelard-Schuman, 1960.

Chapter 2: Loving-Kindness. For this theme treated in a classic work of Musar, see "On Love," in *The Ways of the Righteous* (*Orchot Tzaddikim*). English trans. by Seymour J. Cohen. Jerusalem: Feldheim, 1969, pp. 22–129.

Chapter 3: Compassion. See Samuel H. Dresner, "Compassion," in *Prayer, Humility and Compassion.* Philadelphia: JPSA, 1957, pp. 181–239.

Chapter 4: Love of the Stranger. See Jacob Neusner, *Fellowship in Judaism; The First Century and Today.* London: Vallentine, Mitchell, 1963.

Chapter 5: Shunning of Talebearing. See Norman Lamm, *Faith and Doubt: Studies in Traditional Jewish Thought,* chap. XI, "Privacy in Jewish Law and Theology," for a discussion of how the prohibition of "the evil tongue" affects the treatment of privacy in Jewish Law.

Chapter 7: Courage. For more on Jewish resistance to the Nazis, see Jacob Glatstein and Israel Knox, eds., "Resistance," in *Anthology of Holocaust Literature.* Philadelphia: JPSA, 1969, pp. 275–357.

Chapter 8: Marriage. An excellent anthology is Philip Goodman, *The Jewish Marriage Anthology.* Philadelphia: JPSA, 1965. For a brief introduction to a little-known and less understood Jewish practice which sheds more light on the nature of Jewish marriage, see Norman Lamm, *Hedges of Roses: Jewish Insights into Marriage and Married Life.* 4th ed., rev., New York: Feldheim, 1972.

Chapter 9: Marital Sex. See Norman Lamm, "The Moral Revolution: a Jewish Evaluation," in *Faith and Doubt: Studies in Traditional Jewish Thought.* New York: Ktav, 1971, pp. 247–269.

Chapter 10: Children and Parents. See Samuel Belkin, "Parent as Teacher and Teacher as Parent," in *Essays in Traditional Jewish Thought.* New York: Philosophical Library, 1956.

Chapter 11: The Old. Though little has yet been written on this subject, the following colloquium illuminates some of the contemporary aspects of the problem: Edward E. Klein, Eli Ginzberg, and Michael Wyschogrod, "Conference on the Aged: The Responsibility of the Synagogue, Community, the Rabbi and the Laymen, Towards Its Elders," in *News and Views* (Federation of Jewish Philanthropies of New York, Commission on Synagogue Relations), vol. 3, no. 2, Feb.–Mar. 1970. See also Abraham J. Heschel's celebrated address delivered at the 1961 White House Conference on Aging entitled "To Grow in Wisdom," in *The Insecurity of Freedom*. New York: Farrar, Straus & Giroux, 1966, pp. 70–84.

Chapter 12: Sickness and Death. The study of medical ethics in Judaism by the Chief Rabbi of Great Britain is a classic in the field: Immanuel Jakobovitz, *Jewish Medical Ethics*. New York: Bloch Publishing Co., 1962. An informative work on mourning practices is Maurice Lamm, *The Jewish Way in Death and Mourning*. New York: J. David, 1969.

Chapter 13: Business Honesty. See Leo Jung, *Human Relations in Jewish Law*. New York: Jewish Education Committee, 1967.

Chapter 14: Freedom. More of the heroic writing by Soviet Jews will be found in Moshe Decter, ed., *Redemption; Jewish Freedom Letters from Russia*. Foreword by Bayard Rustin. New York: Conference on Soviet Jewry, 1970. Highly recommended is the classic volume by Elie Wiesel, *The Jews of Silence*. New York: Holt, Rinehart & Winston, 1966; also available in paperback: New York: Signet, 1967.

Chapter 15: Leadership. See the two chapters by the leading Jewish historian: Salo W. Baron, "Law and Ecclesiastical Officers" and "Religious Guidance," in *The Jewish Community; Its History and Structure to the American Revolution*. Philadelphia: JPSA, 1942, vol. 2, pp. 52–168. Elie Wiesel's work on the Hasidic masters, *Souls on Fire,* New York: Random House, 1972, has much to teach about charismatic Jewish leadership.

Chapter 16: Self-Government. See the essay by Samson Raphael Hirsch, "Jewish Communal Life," in *Judaism Eternal: Selected Essays,* translated and annotated with an introduction and biography by I. Grunfeld. Soncino Press, 1959, vol. 2, pp. 97–144.

Chapter 17: Other Religions. For a profound Jewish view on interreligious dialogue, see the brilliant essay by American Orthodoxy's most eminent teacher and thinker: Joseph B. Soloveitchik, "Confrontation," in Norman Lamm and Walter Wurzburger, eds., *A Treasury of Tradition*. New York: Hebrew Publishing Co., 1967, pp. 55–80. An earlier writer on the subject is also worth consulting: Bernard Drachman, "Jewish-Gentile Relations Considered from Jewish Viewpoint," in Leo Jung, ed., *Judaism in a Changing World* (The Jewish Library, vol. 4). London: Soncino Press, 1971, pp. 106–123.

Chapter 18: Nature. See the chapter entitled "The Earth Is the Lord's," in *Judaism and Human Rights* (Milton R. Konvitz, ed.). New York: Viking Press, 1972, pp. 247–274.

Chapter 19: Peace. For a number of discourses on themes indirectly related to peace, see Norman Lamm, "The Contemporary World," in *The Royal Reach; Discourses on the Jewish Tradition and the World Today*. New York: Feldheim, 1970, pp. 111–162.

Index